Go with the River

GO WITH THE RIVER

Mary Wright Shaw

GANDER PUBLISHING INC., PALO ALTO, CALIFORNIA

Although the stories in this collection are autobiographical,
a few names have been changed for the privacy of individuals.

Library of Congress Catalog Number: 96-094901

ISBN 0-9639586-0-7

Copyedited by Rene Lynch, Los Altos, California
Flap copy by Susan Sharpe, Words & Ideas, San Francisco, California
Cover Photograph by Howard Jarvis, Warren, Pennsylvania
Text design and production by Teutschel Design Services,
Palo Alto, California
Jacket design by Robert Aulicino, New York City

Printed in the United States of America

Gander Publishing Inc.
Palo Alto, California

For My Children and My Grandchildren

In Memory of My Mother

Anna Gander at 16 years of age

Acknowledgments

My love and appreciation to my sister, Virginia Wright Buckingham Mitchell, for supporting the publishing of this collection.

My special thanks to friends in the writing and publishing world: Nina Holzer, my editor, showed me the way, and challenged me from the first day I entered her writing class. Alice LaPlante and Joan Wieder, classmates in Stanford University's Continuing Studies Writing Course, bolstered my confidence. Camille Hykes, an editor whom I met at the Bread Loaf Writers' Conference, provided a sensitive, candid assessment of my writing, revealing for me an insight about what was missing. Dorothy Nash, who was always available as a wise consultant.

Sarah and Dennis Teutschel, designers of the interior of my book. Robert Aulicino, cover designer. Howard Jarvis, photographer of the Allegheny River. Susan Sharpe, writer of the cover summary, and Rene Lynch, copy editor.

I am also deeply grateful to my friends who have encouraged me. Jean Gertridge Jones, who early on read everything I wrote until she died two years ago. Beverly Differding, who kept me on course with her steadfast spirit and interest in my writing. Diane Broadwater, who listened and listened to some of my stories even before I wrote them. Gitti Kalkuhl, who read my stories and spurred me on by constantly asking me, "Did you write today?" Dr. Gerald Shefren, who was *there* for my grandbabies, and who gave my baby stories a read. My Stanford golfing friends, who also gave me the gift of reading some of my stories: Emily Garfield, Bernie Lynch, Dorothy Lazier, Linda Kaiser, Nancy Merryman, Gretchen Scott, and Eleanor Walker. Katie Ladd, who accompanied me back to the river in Pennsylvania where my life and writing began. Barbara Moon, Margaret Conroy, and Jeannine Ansell, my cousins, Hazel Sarvis, my mother's friend and bridge partner, Bill Bunk, a high school classmate, and his wife Janyce, who welcomed me home to Warren after so many years.

Table of Contents

About My Stories

My mother used to say, "Go with the river." I felt the flow of the stream when I was a little girl sitting on the bank of Conewango Creek in Warren, Pennsylvania, watching my brother and his friend riding rafts. They used long poles to keep from drifting toward the shoreline and they could only go with the flow, bumping into tangled tree roots worn away by high waters, or crashing into the rocks in the shallows. I could see it was the water's way, always flowing into larger routes, from mountain streams like Ott Run to the brook under the street we lived on, Brook Street, gushing into the creek along Conewango Avenue, and finally merging into the wide Allegheny River down by Pennsylvania Avenue.

Later, in the 1940s, as a student nurse at Massachusetts General Hospital in Boston, I watched the excavation for the White Building, which would expand the surgical service. We were shown an etching of the original hospital, the Bulfinch Building, as it existed in 1821. In splendid simplicity it sat beside the Charles River, and was accessible for patients by boat. Over the years the river changed its course and left the Bulfinch Building high and dry, with land all around for further expansion of the hospital.

Then, as the bulldozers removed the earth for the foundation of the new construction, the massive hole filled with water. For a few months the water seeped in from the Charles River Basin and we were able to visualize the old river route. However, gradually the water found its way back to the river bed.

More recently, on a hike in the Sierra Mountains, a geology student explained a watershed: a place where the land becomes high and dry as a river changes its course. And I was aware that crucial changes in my life were like the watersheds in a river's life.

The stories in this collection are about the process of coping when circumstances seemed insurmountable; or times when I felt abandoned, unable to continue on the route I had been taking. During those times I looked inside myself, reaching for the water of my soul, the core of my being, and found strength and often a new direction. I believe it is one's inner spirit, one's capacity for love, that is the water of the soul that helps find the way. The might of my inner spirit will take me where I need to go; I cannot see it, but this power moves me as the river moves.

My journal gave birth to my stories and served me as a sketchbook serves an artist, priming the pump, getting the story or the picture started, creating the flow of thought and images. For me a journal entry may be about anything—nature, action, memory, dreams—the mind is free. In his *Letters to a Young Poet* Rilke says, *"Go into yourself and see how deep the place is from which your life flows; at its source you will find the answer to the question of whether you must create."* And I discovered that my journal entries triggered the flow of my writing from my gut, from my heart, and from my soul.

❦

Journal Entry: July 7, 1987, Yosemite

Dina and Bridgit and I have come to the mountains to hike and write. We are at 8000 feet elevation by the lower lake. A boat has taken us across Saddlebag Lake to climb the mountain to Steelhead Lake, 2000 feet above. "Wear your sturdy hiking boots," Bridget had said, "the hike will be rough and the shale pieces sharp." I am glad I have listened to her, as I climb over large rocks and granite pieces, putting one foot in front of another, ascending the stone-cluttered shore as it rises up, away from the lake.

As I climb I feel pure peace and quiet. Here, everywhere I look, the air I breathe, the fragrance, the occasional tap of a pine cone falling—all of it—lulls me into a sensitive place. I hear the wind whispering through sparse trees, pine needles singing, and even the occasional bird song tranquil and humble. "Be still and know that I am God" is all around me.

As I follow Dina up the mountain I face another mountain peak, and clinging to the curve of the graceful form is a bundle of snow. The rugged peak is my mother, a pillar of granite, holding me in her bosom. I am the snow, buffeted by the winds of this world. I am alone, cold, desolate. She warms me. I melt. I flow into a lake and I am quiet and peaceful. I am just one stream of water, crashing, flowing, seeking my way. I flow and fall into another even greater more placid lake, full of life. And my spirit is free, the melting snow filling the streams, the lake, the river, and the ocean. I watch my reflection in the shimmering lake and see it dancing above the cascading falls.

Journal Entry: September 5, 1995, Palo Alto

The Baby Dream

I had that dream again last night. It was the baby dream. I had put the baby to bed and time kept going by. I knew that I would have to go upstairs and feed her, but I just couldn't seem to get everything done. I didn't forget about her—I knew that she was probably going to wake up and be hungry—and I needed to go to her. But I kept thinking that she would be O.K.

I was trying very hard to get to her; in fact, I was becoming almost frantic, and I felt so guilty. How could I have a baby and not feed her? I told the people I was with that I needed to feed my baby. I could see her asleep, at least I thought or hoped she was sleeping, but then I visualized her waking up and getting twisted in her bedclothes, and something terrible happening to her. I even wondered if she would survive. I worried that maybe she would starve before I got there. I could see her upstairs in her crib just waiting for me. But then I was cleaning a closet and everywhere I looked there was something I needed to take care of, shoes, lots of shoes—I just couldn't get anything done.

My dream took me to San Francisco, and I was so far away from my baby. I wanted so badly to get home and feed my baby. I had been trying all day long to get to my baby. I knew that someone who doesn't feed a baby is very bad, so I was driving home as fast as I could. I wanted to drive straight home, but for some reason I was taking a different route. I turned onto another high-way—but it seemed as though it was going more away from my house than toward it. In fact, it looked like a dead-end street I had taken before and landed in a neighborhood that I always got lost in. So I turned around, actually backed up a dirt road, and decided to go home the way I usually went. I was now more frantic than ever, even feeling short of breath. I thought I remembered this street because of its curves, but it went down into a section that looked deserted. I passed lots of hilly streets, and as I drove along I knew I had taken another wrong turn. I felt like I'd never get home to my baby.

The next thing I knew I was in a coffee shop with people who seemed to know me. They wanted me to try their chocolate croissants. I stood before the counter and tasted one that was on display. I simply licked the chocolate that was iced on the top. "This is real chocolate," I said. "You always have the best, but I can't have one. I have to go home to feed my baby." And the chocolate taste lingered and I loved it; it was very rich and delicious.

Suddenly I was at home, but it was my old house where I used to live with my children. There were all kinds of people around, some whom I knew and others who didn't register with me. One woman was friendly and she was sitting on a chair beside a bathtub. On the edge of the bathtub was something that looked like a handmade bracelet, or a necklace, perhaps a scarf rolled up very tight. It was just lying there, like it had been tossed aside. I really wasn't sure what it was. I didn't know whether she was showing it to me or not. The bathtub was empty. I woke up, worrying about my baby.

It was four-thirty in the morning.

❦

This reoccurring dream of the neglected baby had come in and out of the depths of somewhere within me over the past several years. Periodically it has returned and I have recorded different versions of it in my journal many times; it seems to hold great importance. I have been concerned and worried about this baby of my dreams, but apparently I have continued to neglect her. However, after this last dream, through the fog, the fragments, and the wisps of the dream, I began to have an awareness of its meaning.

The neglected baby dream had first appeared when I decided to write a collection of stories. Yet, in spite of this decision, I would shove my writing aside because my life was consumed with other projects. But I would not forget about my writing; I wanted to reveal memories and show scenes that were tucked away in my mind, worth preserving, it seemed, like keepsakes concealed in an attic. It was a priority for me, yet it would lose its status whenever a family crisis occurred, or when some other seemingly important project consumed me. Often I would just need to earn some money to pay bills.

Finally, I have made a commitment to write about my river, the river that is my life, a route of aloneness with its currents and watersheds, its rapids and its calms, and the constant flowing. Since I have been writing I no longer have dreams of the neglected baby. The initial story in this collection was an assignment in a writing class: "Write about the first time you had a sense of self."

I think of William Wordsworth's *"the Child is father of the Man,"* echoing Milton's musing, *"The childhood shows the man, As morning shows the day."*

As a child it seemed to me I could feel words—pussy willow, shadow, polliwogs, twinkle, robin—or was it that these feelings surfaced in the poems I heard? I became excited about writing when I won an essay contest in seventh grade; the W.C.T.U., Women's Christian Temperance Union, had sponsored the competition, rewarding the student who wrote the most convincing argument for abstaining from alcohol. The award was a check for $5.00, but I also remember the relief I felt as I revealed my deep feelings with pen on paper, denouncing the use of alcohol, describing the misery it caused. I wrote of small, flat bottles, hidden bottles, alcohol on the breath of a gentle man, warning us children of his change of mood; my mother's boyfriend was an alcoholic. I did not forget that essay, the pure joy of writing.

Later, during my first year at Stanford, my interest in writing was rekindled as I wrote compositions in English class. Again I wrote from experience; I had served in the Army Nurse Corps, and it was after I had given birth to my first baby that I enrolled as a student on the G.I. Bill. (In fact, our baby qualified us for housing in Stanford Village.) My instructor called my writing "real." But my university life was shortened when my husband completed his Master's degree and launched his career; we helped create the postwar baby boom, producing five children, and, except for letters to friends and to my mother, my writing ceased.

Years later, a lifetime later, in the spring of 1987 I sat in the parking lot of Foothill College, coaxing myself to enroll in a writing course. I sat quietly, almost immobile, for nearly an hour thinking to myself that I really couldn't write, so why bother. I thought I should drive away, but truly a spirit inside moved me; I found myself walking down halls, searching for the registration office. I inquired about Mary Jane Moffatt's autobiography writing class, and was notified that it was filled but a new class was available, taught by Burghild Nina Holzer. "She's very good," they said as I filled out my registration form.

During Holzer's first session I almost decided to leave. She gave us an in-class assignment: write about a time you defied authority when you were a child. "What an impossible assignment," I said to a fellow classmate, a woman of my vintage (in her sixties). "That's a stupid assignment—it's generational—when I was young we never defied authority. I never even dreamed of talking back to my mother."

"Nor did I," said my friend. "We never sassed our parents, in fact, discipline was something we counted on."

So I started my story with an argument to the teacher; how this notion, this idea of challenging authority, was not an appropriate subject for people of my age. And a strange thing happened just in the process of writing;

thoughts came into my mind and onto the page. I found myself telling the story of the time my friend Jeanne and I hid in the shadow of trees along the creek while my sister, two years older than I, and her friend Gwen applied Tangee lipstick to our eager lips. I wrote about scrambling up the creek bank and onto the crosswalk, feeling quite beautiful, just as our mother stopped at the intersection. My mother was not very tall and only her head was visible through the window of her sputtering Essex coupe. She looked directly at us as we tried not to look at her; we had been forbidden to paint our faces. But I thought I saw her smile a little as I heard the shifting of gears, and then she called out the window to us, "Sorry I can't give you a ride, girls; I need to go over to East Street School." We stood motionless as she waved and drove away.

When my teacher returned my story she had written in the margin, "See, you not only remembered a time when you defied authority, but you also recalled a lesson about tolerance from your mother." My writing pump had been primed; the more I wrote the more I was able to write, words flowing as freely as my thoughts. I began to keep a journal and writing became a habit; vignettes I called them at first, windows of my life. Scenes appeared in my mind, as videos, and I recorded them.

My father and mother, Thomas and Anna Wright, married 1914

A First Memory

I was four years old, sitting on the front steps of my house on Brook Street. I looked down at the steps—the gray paint was beginning to crack and flake off. The bottom step rested on the concrete walkway that joined the big sidewalk. There were fading chalk marks from last week's hop-scotch before the light rain fell. My sister, Ginny—she was six years old—had taught me how to throw the flat smooth stone, and how to hop on the squares. We had searched out back, in the garden, for just the right stone. This morning it was fun to remember how I had learned to stand on one leg on the hop-scotch square and not touch the line while I picked up the stone. Ginny had told me that I was good at it.

The big oak tree in the front yard shaded the steps. It was late morning and the dirt street was almost dry. Across the road I could see Mrs. Sweeting laying out her bear rugs for an airing on her front lawn. Usually I would run across the street to talk to Mrs. Sweeting's bears, and pet their thick black fur and smooth heads as they lay on the grass. But today I did not want to move from the top step. I could smell the summer—the lilac by the corner of the porch and the lily of the valley in the shadow of the steps—the freshness after the rain. I was thinking to myself, "Jesus must really love me because I'm really good."

I *wanted* to be very kind and love everyone. Mother had been so sad—she was crying. I wanted to do something to help her.

My father had been sick for a long time. Yesterday he had lain in a long dark box with lots of flowers. I stood beside my mother and my sister and my two brothers while the box my father lay in was lowered into a deep straight hole in the ground. I had held tightly to my sister's hand. I could still feel her hand in mine. And we held tightly onto each others' hands afterwards, and told each other that we would be sure to help our mother.

The yellow ice truck came rumbling down the street, but none of us were running after it this morning. Bill, the ice man, was quieter than usual as he walked around to the cellar door. He had a great square of ice on his shoulder and stopped to place a few chips of ice in my hand. Everything was different today—he usually chased us off the truck when we hopped up to get ice chips. We tried to catch them as he chipped the chunks of ice.

I felt the ice melting in my hands. I didn't care about the ice or the bears. I'm still a little girl, I thought, just sitting on the front steps, looking across the street at the silent black bears, but I can *do* something. Inside of myself I was feeling something new, like I was growing up. I felt that I could learn to do many things, that I could really help my mother. I would make a difference in Mother becoming happy again.

John David, Mary, Virginia, Thomas, Jr., 1924

My Sister and I

A pervasive sense of loss clouded my childhood after my father died when I was four years old. Life in our house seemed different from life in the homes of my friends who had both parents. Mainly it seemed to me that my brothers and sister and I were somehow less than whole, even though we had an unusual mother. Yet the need for my father was felt even more deeply during my adolescence. I believe the void in my early childhood was filled by the energy of our family, the caring for one another as we dealt with the necessities of life.

My sister, Ginny, was twenty months older than I, and my mother always wanted us to play together and to be friends. We honored her wish and spent most of our childhood working and playing with each other, dealing with basic tasks every day while creating our own amusement and pleasure. During the hot summers in the small town of Warren, Pennsylvania we relied on our resourcefulness to occupy the long humid days and the warm evenings. We shared household chores with the "boys," our two brothers: Tom, who was two years older than Ginny, and John David, who was two years younger than I. We took turns with the various housecleaning tasks, but Ginny and I always did the laundry.

The Maytag washing machine was in the cellar. There was a laundry chute which deposited the soiled clothing onto the part-earth and part-concrete floor of the cellar. Ginny and I, eleven and nine years old, tackled the task with uncommon fervor, eager to be done with it. We sorted out the wash in the dankness and darkness of the basement, brightened somewhat by the fragrance of the apple bin where the crop of apples was stored for the winter months. My father had planted two Northern Spy apple trees in our backyard when my oldest brother was born. Thirteen years later, the trees yielded an abundance of hard, deep red apples, the kind that lasted all winter. We were afraid of rats who entered the musty cellar through the earth floor, attracted by the apples; we could hear their noises at night. Tom had set a box trap one evening, and in the early morning hours Ginny and I shuddered when we heard the banging of the lid as a rat tried to escape its prison. Although Ginny and I were scared, Tom didn't have the heart to kill the rat so he released it near the creek the next morning. "I let it go, way up by the North Warren swinging bridge," he said, apparently to comfort us.

We tried to make a game of doing the wash, timing ourselves with each task as we ran up the steep cellar stairs to check the minutes on the Big Ben clock on the stove in the kitchen. The Maytag washer swished the clothes and the Fels Naphtha soap peels during the wash cycle, and we cut short this cycle to run the clothes through the hand-turned wringer into the rinse water. We took turns, one of us feeding the wash into the wringer from the rinse water, while the other revolved the handle that turned the wringer, watching the white sheets appear like long flat tongues only to collapse in the bottom of the bushel basket. We used the same water to wash the "coloreds" and hurried the cycle to wring them out into the fresh rinse water. Together we hung the wash on the clotheslines in the backyard.

None of our friends had the chore of doing their family's wash on Saturday mornings. (Gwen Kinkaid's mother did her baking on Saturdays. Then Mrs. Kinkaid washed on Mondays, ironed on Tuesdays, and sewed on Wednesdays. She went to church on Sundays but I never knew what she did on Thursdays and Fridays.) I did know, however, that these wash times were times in my early life when I was alone with my thoughts. Ginny and I had learned to go through the motions of our work in silence; our main goal was just to get finished. Finally, laughing together, we would take down the dry sheets and clothes from the clotheslines to fold. This was the good part, pressing the sheets with the fragrance of lilacs and roses and breezes into our faces as we held them aloft, each of us grasping two corners to fold them evenly so we had to iron only the hems. We placed them in tan bushel baskets with wire handles to carry into the house.

Mother had instilled in us the fact that "any job worth doing is worth doing well—we'll have no halfway work in our house!" And we all knew that Mother always said what she meant and meant what she said. She supported our family by working as the school nurse. Almost all the children in town had been inoculated by my mother for disease immunization. Also, periodically they held out their hands to her for their iodine tablets as they lined up in the health office. (It was something about living in the "goiter belt," and there was not enough iodine in the water in our town, so the health department distributed the yellow-brown pills in the schools to protect our thyroid glands.)

Mother was the only school nurse in town. Everybody knew her and either loved and admired her for her kindness and keen wit or was afraid of her because of her piercing honesty. She set the ground rules in our home, but they were few, and because she worked hard on her job, we kids ran the house. Cousin Minnie, perhaps thinking we were too unsupervised, asked Mother what her philosophy of raising children was. "I intelligently neglect them," Mother said, her intense blue eyes twinkling, as she sat down at the piano and started playing and singing, "Pack up all your cares and woe, here I go singing low, bye, bye, blackbird." And then she added, "You know, Minnie, I just have good kids."

My older brother Tom assumed the authority when it came to the housecleaning. "The girls do the downstairs and the boys will do the upstairs," he said, usually alternating the tasks weekly. Ginny and I ran the carpet sweeper with spurts of energy and took the loose rugs out to the lawn to pound them furiously with a wire carpet beater. We finished our task so quickly that Tom would question our thoroughness by flicking up small grains of dirt with his fingers as he examined the carpet. "Look at that!" he would exclaim. "Not finished—no half-way work in this house!"

Ginny and I, ignoring him, were already on our hands and knees scrubbing the kitchen floor. The orange and white linoleum turned bright under our large yellow brushes and frothy soap. We used furniture polish on the round oak table in the dining room and on the "library" table in the living room. Mother had painted this "library" table black, as well as the rocking chairs with their oak arms. Cully, Mother's boyfriend, had upholstered the seats with a red and black oriental-type fabric, and she was proud of their creative decorating. It was a bewitching room, I thought, at night when the lamp on the table brought the print in the chairs alive. Mother burned incense in that room when she invited her friends for a party or a bridge game. Ginny and I and the boys greeted her guests, usually teacher-friends, and then went upstairs to bed, listening to the voices, rising and falling, and the outbursts of laughter. Mother sometimes played the piano and sang, but on bridge game nights the atmosphere became quiet and serious. Once in a while Ginny and I would smell cigarettes, so we tried to look down the stairway to see who was smoking. It excited us.

Ginny and I shared a double bed on the sleeping porch. The space allotted to each of us, by our designation, was defined by an imaginary line, from the middle brass post at the foot of the bed to the middle post at the head of the bed. These property rights were enforced during the night by muffled admonitions: "Stay on your own side"; "Move your feet—they're touching mine"; "Don't breathe in my face"; or just plain, "Stop breathing!"

Before sleep my sister and I shared thoughts; she always had the answers and felt responsible for me. Early on I believe I allowed her to manage my life as well as her own. I think I deferred to her for the sake of peace, not wanting to argue when she said, "I know what I'm talking about!" She was very knowing when she told me how babies were made, what happened between a man and a woman in bed. And when I asked in disbelief, "How could they do that?" she assured me, "It happens while they're asleep."

In the simplicity of the small town, and the sparsity of material goods in our family, our life was dependent on our imaginations. I learned to daydream. Mother encouraged our daydreaming; her own air castles were filled with music and flowers and money. She loved a party, a circus, a parade, and her garden.

Mother's great joy besides her family was her flower garden. "With sunshine and rain and love they'll bloom," she said as she talked to her roses. It was a prediction she made come true with an abundance of seed catalogues: Burpees, Wayside Gardens, and others. Along with the order sheets, they often covered the dining room table on weekends during the winter months while she planned her garden and ordered seeds. My older brother seemed to think Mother would not be so broke if she did not buy so many seeds.

Mother said she was happiest when she was "broke." "We are not poor; we're simply broke. And when I'm broke I don't have to worry about which bill to pay because I simply can't pay any of them." Often, at the end of a day, she gathered us around her in the living room to build air castles. I snuggled in the corner of the davenport and watched my sister toss her head back and then smooth her hair, as though the wind blew through while she sat in a yellow convertible. I was entranced. Ginny had a lot of determination, and I believe that she, more than I, *believed* that these fantasies would come true.

There were two things that we dreamed of one summer more than anything else. We both wanted a bicycle, but I wanted one even more than Ginny. Tom had one, but the crossbar was too high, so I learned to ride it a short distance by extending my legs under the crossbar and pedaling with the bike held out at an angle away from my body. But Mother was never able to afford the luxury of girls' bikes for Ginny and me. Tom used his to ride to the golf club to caddy, and for his paper route. He always took the money he earned out of his back pocket and put it on the windowsill in the kitchen for groceries.

The other thing that Ginny and I would almost have walked a million miles for was to be able to go to Camp Newatah on Lake Chautauqua for a week in the summertime with our Girl Reserve Group. We knew there wasn't money enough for us to go to camp. But there was a way perhaps to make this dream come true. In the spring the Y.W.C.A. had a contest in town, selling Veterans of Foreign Wars poppies. These were made of red cloth and green wire to pin on a lapel. People could donate any amount of money for a poppy. The two Girl Reserves who collected the most money selling poppies would win one week at camp.

Ginny and I got up early the Saturday morning of the contest. Happy and giggling, we hurried across the wood walkway of the Fifth Street bridge, which stretched across Conewango Creek. Further up the creek, smoke stacks of the refinery stood tall amidst the pristine foothills and released great billows of black smoke. I watched the smoke fade to gray as it filled the sky and slowly dispersed. I listened to the water sloshing against the piles under the bridge, and I tried to be excited about selling poppies.

Although Ginny was almost two years older, there was little difference in our heights. I ran along beside her, as always, proud of my pretty blond sister, her hair perfect in the straight bob with bangs. I felt gangly, skinny, and my mop of brown curls was always falling into my eyes.

"Pull up your socks, Mary."

I yanked them up as I ran along beside her. She glanced over at me.

"Tie knot is wrong."

We stopped running in the middle of the bridge while Ginny tied my tie. "I don't know what you'd do without me," she said, as she tried unsuccessfully to smooth out my unruly hair. She gave me a little shove. "Oh well, it looks O.K. Let's hurry." Last week on the way to school, I had pushed Ginny into the wrought iron fence by the Banghart lawn, and she had to go home to change her dress. It tore when it caught in the gate. For punishment Mother almost kept me home from the poppy sale, but Ginny wanted me along. I was on my best behavior this morning, letting her take charge. I watched us as we ran down Water Street. I could see that the closer we got to the "Y" the faster Ginny set the pace.

"We're going to win, Mary. I know we are. Let's be the first to be in town when the stores open."

I lagged behind, my fingers caught in the curls I was trying to tame, and said, "It's going to be hard to get people to give money because most people don't have any money."

❧

Herbert Hoover had won the election. The Clinger kids from the big white house on the corner of Fifth Street and Conewango Avenue had been singing, "Hail, Hail, Smith's in jail, Hoover's been elected, just as we expected, Hail, Hail, Smith's in jail, what the heck do we care now?" They had chanted this little lyric across the street from the red brick barber shop on Fifth Street just a block away from our house on Brook Street. For one day this tiny building had been the voting booth, and Ginny and I had written AL SMITH, in chalk, all over its outside walls. My mother had thought he might help us have more money if he became president. But it turned out that we were ordered by some powerful person in town to scrub down the red brick walls with soap and water. I felt sorry for Al Smith as his name dissolved in the suds.

Mother would say, "I'm robbing Peter to pay Paul" when she tried to pay her monthly bills. I had seen her bring in the mail from the wrought iron box clinging to the wall of the front porch on our white clapboard house. She pulled open the screen door and walked directly to her desk where she sorted her letters. Those that looked like bills she simply tore right down the center—unopened—into two pieces and dropped them into the wastebasket. Although it did not seem right to do I always knew somehow that it made Mother feel better. There was nothing she could do about them and that was that.

❦

Ginny was out of breath as we reached the iron fence of the Y.W.C.A. "But just think, Mary, if we collect the most money we'll get to go to camp."

A vision of the morning dip flashed in my head— nothing—no, nothing—thrilled me more about Camp Newatah than my fantasy of the morning dip. There were pictures of Girl Reserves and their morning dips on the bulletin board in the "Y" office. I felt the lake water rush past my body as I plunged head first into the morning newness of the silver lake. My head bobbed up. Now I was almost as excited as my sister.

We signed in with Lottie, our Girl Reserve director. She gave Ginny a special pep talk, knowing that she was the most determined girl she had probably ever known. I noticed Ginny's face; she was very serious, biting her lower lip as she wrote her name carefully at the top of her "intake" slip.

"This is the beginning, Mary," she said, pointing to the long column of blank spaces. "We'll fill our cans fast."

I wrote my name on the long sheet of paper and tried to feel like Ginny. I clutched my bouquet of poppies in one hand, picked up the can with the slit in the center in my other hand, ran out of the "Y," and headed for the main part of town.

"Let's meet back here in two hours," Ginny called to me over her shoulder as she started running up Third Street toward the shops.

All up and down Pennsylvania Avenue I walked. "Do you want to buy a poppy?" "Will you please buy a poppy?" "Help a veteran." The things they told us to say. Pennies and nickels and dimes fell into my can, and I became excited at the prospect of filling my can before the two hours were over. When I met Ginny she had already emptied her can, and her name was at the top of the list. She had gone to a "good" area; people had been generous. We continued collecting until noon and the race became close. Ginny had been the leader all morning; her name was still at the top of the list with the highest total of money collected. But on the last tally other Girl Reserves were catching up. I was next to the bottom of the list. Losing heart, I stood on the corner near the Stein's Women's Shop when Ginny raced up to me.

"How can we win, Mary? I may be in second place now, and you're still way down the list." The expectancy in her voice told me she had not given up hope of winning. We had to make it happen.

I had an idea. "Ginny, here are two quarters; a man just put them into my hand instead of into my can. I kept them out so I could put them in your can. And that's what I'll do from now on. I'll hold out my hand instead of the can, and save the money to put into your can. It all goes to the Veterans of Foreign Wars just the same. Let's go!" Ginny stopped in her rush to take off again, and came back to tell me, "Don't forget—after we win this one week we'll figure out how to get another week." (There was going to be another contest for our church group, and the prize would be a week at Camp Newatah. We both loved to even just *say* "Camp Newatah." Ginny was already thinking of the next contest!)

It had taken all day, but now I was on fire; I was as committed to winning this contest as was Ginny. We had come up with an idea that needed all my help. I went into shoe stores, men's stores, dime stores. I hurried, and alive with enthusiasm, I asked everyone in my path and beyond, "Do you want to buy a poppy?" Mr. McGarry in the barber shop stopped me to have his customers fill my hand with coins. "Say, this is Anne's girl; isn't she doing a fine thing?" I lapped up his praise like a kitten at a milk dish and went into the street determined that my sister would win. I met Ginny on the corner and deposited my handful of coins into her can. We raced back to the "Y" at six o'clock, closing time for the contest. When Lottie opened Ginny's can and all the money rolled out she declared, "I do think we have a winner here!" Ginny had won one week at camp.

Two weeks later when the church contest began there could not have been two more dedicated contenders. The goal was to acquire the most points for participation in church functions and group activities. We were given a specific number of points for Sunday School attendance, for Wednesday night prayer meetings, for attendance at Girl Reserve meetings. If a girl assisted in cleaning the Girl Reserve clubhouse over the parsonage's garage, it would yield special credit. I went to all the prayer meetings with Ginny and we helped each other in many community projects. In the end it was the abundance of wild honeysuckle Ginny gathered for the church altar that gave her enough points to win the contest. She made it possible for each of us to go to Camp Newatah for a week; one of our fantasies had come true.

On arrival at camp Ginny and I were assigned to different locations. I was in a six-bed tent on the hill near the woods, while Ginny bunked in a cabin with the older girls nearer the lake. My best friend, Jeanne, was at camp for the first time also, and we were in the same tent. But we signed up for different activities. She was most interested in arts and crafts and badminton, while I chose swimming and hiking. Ginny's favorite activity was nature study—she would spend much time in the woods collecting specimens of flowers and leaves.

Jeanne and I had known each other since grade school and had often felt a sense of courage when we explored new ventures. Just as junior high was a new experience where we liked to test the rules, so it was at a structured camp that we again felt challenged. One day after lunch, during rest period, Jeanne and I decided to explore the area around the lake, perhaps check out one of the amusement parks nearby, so we left camp through the woods to reach a paved road. We were off limits, A.W.O.L., and hitch-hiked a ride with a man who stopped when we waved to him. As we crowded into the front seat beside the smiling, friendly man, I saw several cartons of toilet paper on the back seat. "Are you a toilet paper salesman?" I asked him. He laughed and said, "Yes, I'm taking this to the girl's camp down the road there; Camp Newatah it's called." Before he could shift gears, Jeanne blurted out, "Oh, I forgot, we need to go in the opposite direction." I opened the car door and said, "Thanks, thanks a lot, but we have to go the other way," and I jumped from his car with Jeanne close behind me. We were wearing sailor caps, actually we thought we looked quite jaunty, but we pulled them from our heads so we wouldn't lose them as we ran down the road, our skinny legs taking us swiftly into the sanctity of the bushes and maple trees along the road.

The flirting with danger, the not obeying the rules seemed exciting and fun, but we were eager to get back to camp and giggled our way through the brush and overgrowth of the woods that protected the camp-grounds. Unfortunately our absence had been noted and a counselor spied us when we reappeared at the edge of the campgrounds. It had also been reported that we had been seen on the road by a camp director.

The disciplinary action that resulted should have been a humiliation, but Jeanne and I seemed to relish being ostracized as we scrubbed the wooden floor of the mess hall. The head counselor gave us mops with enor-mous string heads to rinse in the gray metal buckets and wring out by hand. The handles were too long, making it difficult to maintain our balance as we sloshed the suds back and forth. Other campers came by to watch, among them my sister, who was embarrassed and sad that I had fallen from honor. My entire body and mind tingled with an aliveness as the comedy of our awkwardness caused laughter, and we became the center of attraction in that moment. But it was a bitter-sweet moment, and I decided to concentrate on the swimming program for the remainder of my week at camp.

At the closing campfire Ginny won an award, "Ready for Service." And I learned to dive that summer, feeling the depth of the plunge and the buoyancy of ascent, the thrill of being myself.

I never did own a bicycle when I was growing up, but as time went by I was tall enough to ride Tom's bike properly. As I rode my brother's bicycle, I saw myself free, in control, alive, alone with my thoughts. I was an adventurer in a tan poplin raincoat, the collar turned up, caressed by the breeze and the fine mist of the summer rain.

Mary, 1937

Campaign Card of Ben Kinnear, 1936

Going to Boston

We were on the way to Union Station in Washington, D.C. where I would board a train to take me to Boston to begin my nursing education. It was 1938 and I had visited my sister, Virginia, and her four roommates in their apartment at 1910 K Street. I had never had so much fun in my life, and now they were all taking me to the station to say goodbye, to give me a send-off. Ginny was nineteen years old, I was seventeen, and we had not seen each other for almost a year. Ginny had completed a one-year secretarial course at Marjorie Webster School in Washington, a highly touted school of its kind, and our mother was proud that she had qualified for a job in the Library of Congress.

Mother had thought it was important for me to have a vacation with my sister. The correspondence from the Training School for Nurses at Massachusetts General

Hospital stated that I would not have any time off until I had spent a year at the hospital in *training* (a term that always made me feel like I was being disciplined to jump through hoops). Most of the student nurses in my class were from Massachusetts and they would be able to go home when they had a Saturday afternoon along with a Sunday morning off duty. But because I lived in Pennsylvania, at least ten hours away by train, such trips would be impossible for me. Nor would I be able to travel home when my single long day for the year was announced. Somehow those rules about time off had not concerned me until now, when only a few minutes were left before getting on the train to Boston. I had not given much thought to the daily routine of a nurse, instead I had been consumed with fantasies about leaving home, getting out into the world. Why must I go to Boston when I had fallen in love with Washington, D.C.?

Ginny and her friends had introduced me to all kinds of activities absolutely foreign to me. I went to fraternity parties and experienced the advances of passionate young men far beyond anything I had known in my small home town. We went to outdoor concerts, and one evening my sister's roommate, Smittie, actually won a jitterbug contest. I learned to dance with more vigor than I had ever dreamed possible. On a Saturday we went to Bethesda, Maryland, and spent the day on a luxurious old schooner, cruising on Chesapeake Bay with some Navy midshipmen. It was a relaxed, all-day party. I felt awkward and out of place at first, but I wore a pretty tan linen dress (Mother had splurged to buy it for me at Metzgar and Wright's department store) and it bolstered my self-image. At least I thought I looked O.K. At the end of the day I was hooked on parties, a nascent playgirl.

Washington was a pleasant, balmy city in late August, and we spent many evenings lounging on the roof of the apartment house, just cooling off, talking and thinking about what to do next. I wondered why I was going to Boston. I wondered why I had not considered going to Washington, D.C. like my sister. I wondered also why I was going into nurses' training.

I had wanted to go to college; I had visions of being a doctor. Science and math were my strong subjects in school, and my mother had wanted me to go to college like my oldest brother, Tom. He had two scholarships to Penn State, and with the money he made on summer jobs and at school, he was "working his way through college." But there were no scholarships for girls; if the family did not have enough money, it was almost impossible for a girl to go to college. In fact, it wasn't considered that necessary for a girl; she would more than likely get married, bear children, and keep house. It had been a struggle for Mother to meet the expense of secretarial school for Ginny. But now Ginny had a career, and planned to send me spending money while I was in training.

I remembered how my mother had always had a certain sadness whenever we talked about my applying to nursing schools, even after Dr. Schmell, the school doctor, suggested that studying to become a nurse was a good way for me to get an education. "In those first-rate hospital training schools like M.G.H.," he said, "the student nurses learn on the job, like you did, Anne, only they have Harvard doctors and Columbia doctors in charge, so it's much more educational than what you experienced in this little hospital in Warren. The nurses get exposed to the finest medical people in the country, probably in the world—so while they supply the nursing hands for the hospital they receive their education, almost by osmosis." I understood the term osmosis, and did not believe it was possible to just soak up a lot of knowledge in Boston, but it was an opportunity for me to leave my home town and go to a big city.

Still my mother had her doubts, and said to me, "I really wish there was another way—you should be going to college—nursing is so much plain hard, messy work, and probably not that much education over the course of the three years, no matter who the doctors are." Mother knew because she had been through it; she had graduated from Warren General Hospital when she was nineteen years old.

My friends, Betsy and Jeanne, whose fathers could afford to send them to college, were making their plans. College catalogues arrived in the mail at their houses and we pored over the pictures of dormitories and campuses of the University of Pennsylvania, Temple University, Drexel, and Oberlin. I particularly liked the ivy-covered brick buildings. We fantasized about living in the dormitories; the catalogues showed diagrams of student rooms. Fascinated by the wide expanse of lawns and walkways between buildings, I felt myself being there; I sensed the excitement, smelled the trees and flowers, and thought I even tasted the food. And I was intrigued by the course offerings, and the libraries. I thought about all the books; in one catalogue there was a suggested reading list. On the list was *Plutarch's Lives.* Who was Plutarch? I wondered.

But I knew that in order to leave home and go away to school I had to concentrate on writing letters to the nursing schools Dr. Schmell had recommended. They required an essay about why I wanted to be a nurse; I really did want to be a nurse, I told myself, not because I *wanted* to be a nurse, but because I thought it was the only way I could get an education. I filled out applications and wrote essays and letters about why I desired to become a nurse, and the more I corresponded with hospital training schools, the more I accepted the idea of a nursing education. At least it was a path I could take. "I like people," I wrote, "and I want to help them." And that was true; it was probably the most reasonable grounds, the one justification, for me to become a nurse.

Both Massachusetts General Hospital in Boston and Columbia Medical Center in New York City notified me that I was accepted into their programs, but I could not enter until I was seventeen years old. I had skipped fifth grade and graduated from high school a year early so had to wait a year to go into nurses' training. I decided to go to M.G.H. the following year; my mother thought Boston was a better place for me to live than New York City.

❦

I had never been able to figure out why the school principal and my mother decided that I should leave fifth grade early and move on to sixth. But I recall being sent to summer school to learn fractions so I could skip the last half of fifth grade and pass on to sixth grade in Beatty Junior High School when it opened in the fall. It is one of the videos recorded in my mind's eye; my first few weeks at Beatty School were a string of long days which I would never forget. It was a brand new school that accommodated sixth and seventh grades. My sister and I arrived together, and we immediately parted to find our homerooms. The halls were wide and light, fragrant with the lingering scent of new wood and fresh paint. The vastness of the new building created an abundance of empty spaces, and I felt another emptiness center inside of me as I walked down the long hallway to my homeroom. I felt as though I was the only one walking down the hall, but there were others hurrying past me. Finally reaching my homeroom I headed toward a seat in the back row. Long, charcoal-gray blackboards lined the front and side walls. They were smooth, untouched, and the natural wood trays for chalk were almost as white as the chalk. The erasers in the trays were thick with new velvety gray felt. I picked up an eraser and ran my fingers across the soft surface. It had never been used to erase. I thought of Jefferson School and the worn-out erasers, my cousin Barbara, my friends, Phyllis Ingalls and Mary Spies, and wondered how they liked Mr. Carlson, the fifth grade teacher. We had giggled about him a lot; we thought he was cute. I wished they were here with me to at least see my homeroom teacher when she walked into the room for the first time. I would have different teachers every period in different rooms.

I slid back and forth on my slippery seat at my new desk, looked around, searched for a familiar face. I thought about Donald Yaeger when he moved into the house behind us on Conewango Avenue. "The new kid" we called him, while he watched us from afar, almost like he was afraid of us. None of my friends were in this seemingly untouched place. I crossed my saddle shoes at my ankles and looked down at them; my feet ached because my oxfords were a size too small, a situation I had created because I didn't want my feet to look too big.

My sister, Ginny, would now be only one grade ahead of me; going to classes on the second floor with all her seventh grade friends who had moved with her into this *wonderful* new school. She would invite me to join them for lunch, but I could tell that she felt it was her duty. "Thanks, Ginny," I had said, "I'd rather eat with some of the kids in my class." But no one asked me, and mainly I felt scared and almost like not even going to school. Once I got there I really wanted to go home, but I knew I had to stay.

At lunchtime I sat on a bench outside of the long gymnasium room and ate alone. I had tried to find a bench where no one would see me alone. Mother never knew how much I missed all my friends whom I had left in the fourth grade, how I missed Jefferson School, and how I even missed Miss Johnson, the principal, who had called Mother in for a conference when I hit John Fenstermacher when he spilled my ink. Now I'd probably never see my friends, or Miss Johnson, or John Fenstermacher again.

The course of my life changed when I was hurried on to the new school. Beatty School, a two-story brick building, sprawled over flat low land. In the spacious meadow-like setting broad lawns of mowed grass merged into the wild high grasses along Conewango Creek. In a town where the water ran through in brooks and creeks and a river, and bridges were plentiful, one lived with moving water—heard its voice, felt its soft moisture, saw its constant flow as it crashed against rocks along the edges, always limited by the steep bank. Alone during much of the first year of junior high school, I developed a kind of self-containment and introspection. I still stand by a creek or a river and think about the water I watch—finding its way to a measureless, broader body of water.

❧

During the year I waited to go to Boston to enter nurse's training I was on a dry plateau, a kind of watershed of aloneness. One of the brightest lights on the otherwise dim horizon were those evenings I played mah-jongg with Betsy Kinnear and her family. On one such occasion, while we were gathered around the heavy oak dining room table arranging the tiles for the game, Mr. Kinnear said to me, "Your mother tells me you'll be at home this year, waiting to go to nursing school. I wonder how you'd like to work for me?" It was difficult to believe what I was hearing, and I was almost speechless, but I was comfortable in the presence of Mr.

Kinnear. He was a tall, big man who seemed to listen when he talked with Betsy's friends, and especially to me. I told him that I'd like to, but I didn't think I could be of much help in an office. Mr. Kinnear was the Registrar and Recorder of Warren County and had a large office in the court house. He looked at me across the table and said, "Your mother tells me you've had a semester of typing—and Betsy had the same. I want you both to work for me this summer. She goes to college in the fall, but you can continue until you go to Boston. In no time you'll become an expert. We record every legal document of this county in our record books."

I said, "Oh, I'd love to do that, Mr. Kinnear, if you think I can," and inside I was nearly bursting with joy— I felt so good I could almost fly. I had a job.

Walking home on the darkened street I knew a very important thing had happened. I could smell the spring blossoms in the air and feeling the chill of the evening I pulled my sweater snugly around my body. Not only did I have a job for that year until I could go into nurses' training, but I had a new feeling of self-confidence. My entire being was alive—I felt pretty and secure. Everything in that night was clear—the half moon, the stars, and my awareness that Mr. Kinnear really liked me, and even more—he seemed to really care about what happened to me. It was like the fantasy I had about my father. I knew in that moment that I would always have love for this man who seemed to care about me the way I dreamed my father would. From my early memories along with stories my mother told about my father, and from his photographs, I created fantasies, imagining what it would be like if he were alive.

During that year, while I worked in Mr. Kinnear's office, our friendship flowered with his continued approval of me and my work; as long as Ben Kinnear lived, I knew he would be the first person I'd go to see whenever I returned home on visits. After his term as Registrar and Recorder he had a stationery store, and I would walk into the shop's front door on Liberty Street. His greeting, his welcome, was constant. Always his eyes would light up as though he liked what he saw, and he would listen to me, ask if there was anything I needed, as though I were an important person. Betsy's father with his uncommon kindness helped me create the image of my father which throughout my life has nurtured me.

Not only did the job with Mr. Kinnear provide remuneration and fill in the void before I went to Boston, but it also alerted me to the monotony of life in an office. In the beginning I typed deeds and leases very slowly on the great pages for the record books. In a few months I was a speedy typist, and during those months I also learned that I would never want to work in an office all day.

Bored with the routine, the sameness—one large legal ledger after another became thicker with my typed pages—indeed I felt lucky, extraordinarily excited, when I filed my last document and skipped down the steps of the court house.

I had escaped to a new freedom, I thought, when I said goodbye to my mother in the Warren, Pennsylvania depot and boarded the train for Boston, via Washington, D.C. I heard the whistle as the train followed the bend around the Allegheny River and picked up speed as we left town. Whenever I hear a train whistle, the image of the railroad and the river come to mind; for me it is soulful.

❧

Washington, D.C. began to sparkle in the late evening, and from the roof of Ginny's apartment building I could see the Capitol, bathed in light, and the reflection of the Washington Monument in the pool of water. I watched the orderly traffic moving around the circular streets, and I thought of my home town; it seemed so far away. Boston seemed even farther away, and yet I knew I must go there; they were expecting me to begin the probationary period. During those first four months of the three years of nurses' training I would be judged as to my fitness for continuing in the program.

Ginny said, "You'll like it, you really will!" And she shared with me how difficult it was for her when she had first arrived at Marjorie Webster School in Washington, out in Rock Creek Park. "Friends!" she said. "Mary, it's the new friends you'll make that'll help you like it." I loved Ginny for her eagerness to make me happy about going to Boston.

We drove to the train station in the blue convertible which was the joy of her roommate, Camilla. The top was down, and Ginny and I and her other apartment mates were nearly spilling out as we sped through the streets of Washington, D.C. I wanted to stay in Washington and continue to participate in the freedom that I had found so exhilarating. But I knew I must go to Boston when we reached the depot.

The stationmaster looked at my ticket, pointed out the gate where my train waited. My sister and her friends, talking excitedly, making a point of celebrating my departure, hurried along beside me. I was taking a night train; Mother had insisted that I take the sleeper so that I would arrive rested. I had thought I should take the coach and sit up all night because it was much less expensive, but Mother had said, "Absolutely not! You're going to go in style." As we approached the long line of Pullman cars a porter greeted us. "Com'on," he said. "Y'all can climb right in with your friend. There's lots of time to get her settled." We clambered up the high metal steps and followed him through a door to a hallway until he stopped and pulled open some heavy drapes. Ginny and her friends exclaimed over all the comforts—the little toilet and washroom. They pounded on the berth and said, "How swell, Mary, you'll be able to sleep all the way to Boston!" Their enthusiasm and excitement about my trip buoyed my spirits until abruptly the whistle blew. We heard the conductor's megaphone voice calling out, prolonging the words, "All aboard!" In one big surge they all hugged and kissed me, hopped off the train, and stood alongside, laughing and calling good luck to me.

I watched my sister wipe away a tear while waving vigorously as the train backed out of the Washington station. The porter, standing near, waved with me; he was quick to say, "I'll make sure you have a good trip. Just let me know when you want your bed made up, Miss." For a minute I didn't know what he was talking about— my thoughts were still on vacation with my sister and her friends. Soon Camilla would be driving them away from the depot to the Hot Shoppe for a milkshake and fried clams.

I slept fitfully that night; I felt the rhythm of the wheels as they rolled over the tracks, and heard the train whistle signal our arrival and departure or simply a passage through towns. Often throughout the night I raised the shade and saw the darkened houses as we steadily went northward. It was about 5:30 A.M. when the porter alerted me, "Time to get up, Miss, we'll be in Boston in one-half hour." Suddenly I was wide awake, reaching for my clothes. I hurried, afraid the train would arrive in the station and I would not be dressed.

I pulled back the curtains, and could see only train tracks on both sides. Through the gray mist of early dawn, scrubby trees, vacant lots, and factory buildings passed by and disappeared from view. I could not believe that we had gone through New York City while I was asleep. I had wanted to wake up and just take a peek at it. Now I couldn't even see Boston; more tracks appeared, other trains alongside. The porter told me we were pulling into the South Station. "They serve breakfast there," he said, and I realized I was hungry.

The porter opened the door of the Pullman car and lowered the steps. "There y'are, Miss; you have a good day now," he said as he handed my suitcase to a redcap and told him to show me where I could have breakfast. "Just follow him," he said giving me a little salute. He had watched over me, and as I handed him the coins— the money Ginny had tucked in my pocket, saying "this's for the porter at the end of your trip"—I suddenly felt completely alone for the first time since leaving Washington.

I walked beside the quiet Pullman cars, finally passing the engine, which still huffed and puffed, emitting train smells, like a spent old man, steaming and sweating.

Inside the depot people slept on long, dark wooden benches. I followed the redcap until we arrived at the restaurant in the corner of the voluminous cold, damp station. The aroma of breakfast cooking and the bright lights awakened me—cheered me—as I tipped the redcap and sat down at a table with my suitcase resting against my leg. When a waitress appeared I ordered a stack of pancakes with syrup, and hot chocolate; pancakes reminded me of home.

Fortified with food I was eager to find my way to the hospital. I brushed off my navy blue Knox hat and adjusted it on my head, mirroring myself in the restaurant window. It was a classic hat, had a lot of style, I thought. I pulled the brim down in the front and slightly angled it over my right eye, smoothed my hair that curled up under and around the turned-up brim in the back. Mother and I had gone to Jamestown, New York to buy it. I had brought along the Knox hat box for small items, but mainly for the looks; Ginny and I thought I looked very chic with it. And I also carried an old tennis racquet, although I scarcely knew how to play, and had a *Time* magazine tucked under my arm. I thought I probably still looked quite a bit like a small town girl, but I had a lot more confidence since I had visited Ginny and her friends.

I waited until almost nine o'clock before I went into the Boston morning to summon a taxi, not to arrive too early on registration day.

"Where to, Miss?" the taximan asked me. "The Rotunda of the Mass General Hospital on Fruit St.," I replied, as if I really knew where I was going. I strained to look everywhere as the taxi rattled over the dirty, crooked, cobblestoned streets, passing dilapidated groups of buildings before emerging into what appeared to be the main part of the city. A policeman on horseback directed traffic near an intersection that bordered two parks. I recognized the Boston Commons from photographs, and as the taxi turned right on a street with wrought iron fences bordering the sidewalk I saw the sign, Arlington Street. We passed the Public Gardens, still brilliant with summer flowers. A few minutes later, going down Charles Street, I watched for number 92, because it was the address of student nurses during their probationary period; it was the nurses' home where I would live. The taxi driver said, "There it is, Miss," and pointed to a three-story frame building, adjoining some small shops and an attractive old hotel with gold lettering inscribed over the entrance, *The Lincolnshire*. I admired these quaint sights of Boston, delighted that I had discovered 92 Charles Street, my living quarters, on my initial taxi ride in Boston, when abruptly we made a right turn and seemed to be in a dreary part of the city. "We're going around Beacon Hill," the taxi driver said, "and we'll turn left up here and then you'll be at the hospital." I was not surprised with the sudden change of scenery; I had seen maps of Boston and the location of the hospital and knew it was on the fringe of one of the largest tenement districts in the city, the North West End. A few blocks away at the foot of the decaying side of Beacon Hill were several burlesque houses, including the Crawford House and the Old Howard. Yet, on the other side of the hospital, patients had a clear, broad view of the Charles River. The sights and sounds of my first ride through Boston resonated within me; I was in the current of life, going with the flow of it, and I was eager and excited when we parked in front of the Rotunda, the entrance of the Massachusetts General Hospital.

That first morning I was introduced to Eleanor Smith, who would always be one of my best friends. She was accompanied by her mother and two sisters. They had come from Lowell, Massachusetts on the train. "You looked so sophisticated when you walked into the Rotunda," said Eleanor later. "Your hat, the *Time* magazine and that tennis racquet—was I ever impressed!" They invited me for lunch at a restaurant on Newbury Street; everyone ordered chicken salad sandwiches, including me. Voraciously hungry, I bit into the creamy sandwich and the filling oozed down my chin. Mopping up my face with the cloth napkin, I looked around the table and saw Mrs. Smith and her daughters carefully attacking their sandwiches with forks. They were trying not to watch me, but they seemed to smile as they ate. Embarrassed, I explained to them, "You know, in Pennsylvania we all eat our sandwiches with our hands!"

They never forgot my comment, and always when I went to Lowell on an overnight with Eleanor they would tell the story about the Pennsylvania girl's first meal in Boston. That luncheon became history, a delightful reminder of the past, when the daily labor and solemnity of nurses' training became a reality for all of us.

*Mary, student nurse at Massachusetts General Hospital,
on graduation day, 1940*

Relief Duty

I was in my second year of nurse's training in Boston. It was 1939 and the harsh days of early winter were warning us of the long, snowy months to come. The bitter winds blowing off the Charles River Basin whistled in and around the 100-year-old Thayer House where the student nurses lived. We went on duty through underground tunnels—a network connecting the buildings of the Massachusetts General Hospital, one of the oldest and most prestigious hospitals in the world. The famed Bulfinch Building was the original hospital constructed in 1811. It was a beautiful simple building, crowned with a dome. The amphitheater within the dome had been the site of the first public demonstration of anaesthesia in 1853 and became known as the Ether Dome. The surgical wards were housed in Bulfinch, where I began my assignment of relief nurse. I was eighteen years old. In those days a young woman could enter a hospital's training school for nurses after completing high school. The three-year course was taught and supervised by graduate nurses and doctors; student nurses learned while caring for patients in the hospital.

Ever since my name appeared on the new roster in the Nursing Office I had been apprehensive about my first evening on the relief shift. I would be in charge of an open ward of thirty-two patients, all male patients. I would be the only nurse working on Ward 28 from 3 P.M. to 11 P.M., in fact I would be the only *person* assigned to the ward for those eight hours. Why do they call it the "relief" shift? I asked myself. It seemed to me that it was the one shift of duty where the nurse really needed some kind of relief. But on the other hand, it could be the time of day when the patients needed to be relieved of the rigors of the "day" shift.

During the day shift, 7 A.M. to 3 P.M., doctors examined patients, medical students and interns took medical histories, lab technicians tied tourniquets and drew blood. Orderlies crouched over gurneys, holding their patients steady, and steered them down long corridors in and out of clattering elevators to the x-ray and operating rooms. There were several nurses assigned to the regular day shift; during this duty all first- and second-year student nurses were put through their paces under the strictest supervision of senior and graduate nurses. The main feature of the day took place—Grand Rounds of the Surgical Service, during which interns, residents, visiting surgeons, accompanied by the Chief of Service, stopped at each bedside in an atmosphere of silence, bordering on awe. The student nurses worked quietly on the fringe of the open ward as the stream of white-coated men flowed from patient to patient. The head nurse—immaculate in her white starched uniform, her white cap bearing the one-inch-wide black velvet ribbon, and on her breast a gold pin with hospital seal, declaring her a graduate nurse—walked behind as she escorted the surgical rounds. At the bottom of each patient's bed was a medical chart which she presented to the intern, who then gave it to the resident. The medical hierarchy was vividly imprinted on the psyche of every observing student nurse. When the Chief of Service appeared we always stood in our respectful silence, and gave him almost holy status.

I had been slow to grasp this concept of superiority. I almost failed my first test in Nursing Arts because I skipped one question. "Why must the student nurse step back for the graduate nurse, and the graduate nurse step back for the intern?—give an example." It had seemed to me an unimportant question so I had skipped it to get on to more serious problems. When my exam was corrected and returned to me there were bold question marks in red ink marching across the space below the unanswered question, followed by a reprimand, in red ink, by Miss Martha Ruth Smith, the Nursing Arts instructor: "This omission is the most blatant insubordination I have ever experienced in an examination!" I was instructed, in red ink, to report to her office before I returned to duty the next day.

I will always remember that day. It was raining outside so I went underground through the tunnel, feeling like a prisoner in a dungeon. Mainly I was horrified that I had forgotten to go back and answer that question. The answer was obvious: "Always defer to those who have more knowledge because in a hospital it is a matter of life and death." I did not realize I had forgotten until I saw all the red ink. I was afraid I would be suspended from nurses' training. My friends, Eleanor and Barbara, failed to cheer me up. (Miss Johnson had summoned Eleanor once for wearing rouge. "You will not disgrace the M.G.H. uniform by painting your face!" she had scolded her. But when she could not scrub off the blush, Elly's natural Irish ruddy color, she had apologized.) But we feared that I would be suspended. Had I committed a real offense?

"You really didn't *do* anything, Mary; it was what you *didn't* do. She can't expel you." Eleanor was adamant, but she shook her head as though to make some sense of it. We were all worried; we had no idea what would happen. Barbara, her face pale and sad, remembered her last encounter with Miss Smith. She had told her if she wore lipstick again she would be suspended until the February class was admitted. "I just wish you'd answered that question," said Barbara.

As I approached Miss Smith's office, I flexed my muscles and walked straight and told myself that I had been toughened up as a probie. I would not be afraid of Martha Ruth (privately we all called her by her first two names). But as I stood before her, hot tears burned my face and my small voice said, "I forgot to go back and answer that one." She peered at me over her wire-rimmed reading glasses, her cap perched at an angle on her nest of brownish-gray hair, and for a fleeting second I thought she looked away, that she was not so intense, but then she drew her shoulders stiffly against the back of her chair. She examined me from the top of my cap to the tops of my shoes. I straightened my feet, holding them close together, and I stiffened my neck, my head held high. I did not move. Then she stood up and walked toward me. I thought she was going to put her hand on my shoulder, but she didn't. Instead she stopped only inches from me. I felt her closeness as she clasped both hands behind her back and said, "I believe you, but remember there's no place for arrogance among our nurses. You may go now, Miss Wright."

Although I was free to leave her office I felt less free than before. Eleanor and Barbara and I became expert steppers-back. At least I certainly went through the motions required of me. I wanted desperately to make something of this opportunity to become a nurse.

I hurried through my late lunch in the almost empty dining room preparing for my first round of the relief shift. On my way to my room to get dressed for duty I stopped at the hospital laundry in the basement. "Here you are, Nurse," a laundry aide said, and tossed the bulky package of starched uniforms onto the counter. He pointed to the message scrawled on the brown-paper wrapping: two blouses held in sewing room to mend seams.

"Pick 'em up tomorrow, Nurse, they were really split open." I shrugged my shoulders, bulging now under the sweater Mother had sent for my birthday. It's that heavy starch diet they feed us, I thought. When they fitted me I weighed 120 pounds, which was just right for my five feet six inches height; now I'm 135. I felt like crying. I was splitting my seams. And inside myself there was also a pounding, a straining to escape.

Alone in the tunnel, my rubber-heeled shoes felt heavier than usual. I wanted to flee, to go back home. Yet I knew I had come to Boston to get an education. I had lived all my life in a small town in Pennsylvania on a street where a brook ran under and emptied into Conewango Creek which flowed into the Allegheny River. I dreamed of going to a big city by the ocean, but mainly I came to Boston because my mother had said, "If you're going to be a nurse I want you to be a good nurse so you need to go to the best hospital that will accept you." She was proud that they wanted me at M.G.H. I thought about Regina Morganwood. She had been at the court house for fifteen years, typing deeds and leases in great record books. I had been lucky to have a typing job there while I waited to go into nurses' training. Often in concert with the tapping of keys I had heard Regina say, "I think I'm getting in a rut; I wish I had something else to do." Coming out of the tunnel into the basement of the nurses' home, I reminded myself of the relief I felt when I left my job in the court house, and escaped from the tiresome tedious task of typing deeds and leases and wills on the great pages of legal ledgers. I was glad I had "something else to do."

I stepped quietly as I climbed the dark stairway of Thayer House, knowing that Nona and Irene were trying to sleep because they had been assigned night duty, the 11 P.M. to 7 A.M. shift. The uncarpeted stairs and long narrow wooden hallways creaked with almost every step. My room, number 29, was on the second floor. I opened the door to its pathetic tidiness. My bed was neatly made and the chair beside it unencumbered. It was a brown wooden chair, straight and uninviting. (Sometimes Van Gogh's painting flashed into my mind—his room in Arles—and I thought we had similar sparse rooms, but Van Gogh's was colorful and not at all tidy.) A single light bulb hung from the ceiling on a twisted brown cord. The one window was long and narrow, and through it a single tree branch cast a dark shadow on the white bedspread. An imposing chest of drawers against the wall opposite the bed was so close I could sit on the bed, pull open the drawers, and put away my starched laundry.

I took a quick bath in the long narrow bathtub in the long narrow tub room. Everything about Thayer House was long and narrow. I splashed my armpits with the special antiperspirant the pharmacy had prepared for student nurses. ALCL2 was written on the label with instructions: apply generously and allow to dry completely (so it would not eat the fabric of our uniforms). Miss Sally Johnson, the Superintendent of Nurses, had issued the order for its use. She was a formidable, impeccable, white-haired woman whose very presence was a voluminous storm cloud. Our black-and-white checked uniforms were particularly prone to dark-colored ovals under the arms. Miss Johnson did not want anyone to see her sweating nurses sweat.

I pulled on my black cotton stockings and fastened them to the garter belt I had bought at Filene's basement, just across the Boston Commons on Tremont Street. Thank heavens, I thought, as I shoved my feet into my polished black shoes, Eleanor had found an efficient style of garter belt to hold our stocking seams straight. Eleanor had a broad Boston accent. I loved the way she pronounced "gaarta" belt.

Donning an M.G.H. student nurse's uniform was a complicated process involving a large number of safety pins. I pinned the starched collar and cuffs to my uniform blouse, lined with muslin, form-fitted, made in the hospital sewing room to fit only me. I was conscious of my body blossoming in the snug blouse, and experienced the pleasure of the feeling, almost a tingling with nipples erect, but not for long. Around the waist of my checked full skirt I secured the two-inch-wide stiff belt with large safety pins. Then I pinned to the stiff belt, front and back, the heavily starched white bib which modestly covered my bosom. The stiff belt, made of cotton webbing, was the keystone of the entire uniform; it held it all together. Finally I stood before my mirror, adjusted my white starched apron, and pinned my cap on my windblown bob. In full uniform I felt like a creation of cleanliness, modesty, and stiffness. Ready to tackle my first evening of relief duty, I drew the charcoal gray cape around my shoulders and headed for the tunnel that would lead me to the Bulfinch Building.

The windows of the great double doors of Ward 28 were cloudy with steam. The surgical wards of the ancient structure were heated with battered noisy radiators. In the center of the enormous room was the Nurses' Station, a large desk, where a cluster of day nurses were recording their notes. I looked at the rows of patients in tightly made beds and felt like one of the beds.

"Guess you want to get started with this report, Miss Wright," the head nurse, Miss Donavan, said. She beckoned me aside. "Glad you came early, more time to meet this crowd." She spoke in a soft, flat voice, through white, crooked teeth, and my eyes followed the sweep of her hand as she invited me to take in the rows of beds in one circular gesture.

Donnie, as her friends called her, had been head nurse on Surgical 28 for ten years and word had it that she "mothered" all her patients. She expected them to receive optimum care, and would sometimes spend extra time breaking in a new relief nurse. I felt lucky for that. Her stocky figure filled her unyielding white regulation uniform, still immaculate after a day's work, but her ruffled cap was slightly lopsided on her limp blond hair, which was pulled into a bun at the back of her head. She tucked the stray strands of hair behind her ears and secured her cap pins as we walked from patient to patient. She fluffed up a pillow, filled a water glass, straightened a spread, identified patients, like my mother walking around her flower garden, acknowledging every plant: an appendectomy, a cholecystectomy, an inguinal hernia, an ileostomy, a subtotal gastrectomy, etc. until we had circled all thirty-two beds.

"We need to do the narcotic count together in the medicine closet," she said. "It's required on change of shifts." As she drew me into the medicine closet, similar to a telephone booth with windows on all sides, she whispered, "This has been a terrible day, Miss Wright; you have one empty bed. We had an 'Allen Street,' Mr. Coan in bed 5." Neither the word death nor any of its derivatives were ever uttered in the hospital. It was routine with the administration to avoid the term: we always reported that a patient was discharged to Allen Street. (The morgue was on Allen Street.) Allen Street was a dismal narrow street behind the main hospital. Thayer House where I lived was also on Allen Street.

Miss Donavan bit her lower lip, and brushed back a tear as she continued her report. "It was peritonitis," she said. "We moved him out in his bed. We tried to make it look like we were taking him to surgery but most of the patients, those in that end of the room anyway, they just knew—they felt something—we couldn't help it." She started counting the morphine grs. ⅙, and handed me the vial, morphine grs. ⅛. As I counted out the tiny white pills on filter paper, she continued, "Now don't be worried. I can see you're nervous, this being your first relief, but all I can say is just keep going and don't stop and you'll get everything done before the night nurse shows up." Our numbers checked, and then we held up the bottles of paregoric and tincture of opium to check the meniscus of each—recording the fluid level.

Trapped steam hissed and hammered in the radiators along the walls under large windows. I thought of our sitting room back home on Brook Street and the flames quietly licking the back of the stove, and how I might go over to the Kinnears on Third Street in the evening and play mah jongg with Betsy and her father, where calming, quiet heat rose from the coal furnace through iron grates in the floor. I wished they could see me in the medicine closet now. How my life had changed in one year!

"I've verified these." Miss Donavan snapped the tiny bottles into their slots. "Now let's just stay here a minute so I can tell you about that Mr. Genoa in bed 10. They've had enough going on today." She turned her head toward the rows of men we could see through the closet window, "and I don't want to stir up any problems. But I'm troubled about Mr. Genoa. He may not make it either. He's a subtotal gastrectomy, and he's old and his prognosis is poor. He's on suction, it keeps clogging, and he's running a fever. Doctor Middleton is on call and he said he'd come back after dinner to check the Wangensteen again."

She ushered me out of the medicine closet, locking the door after her. Then she handed me the key on a chain, attached to a narrow cylinder of wood about one inch in diameter and six inches long. "Tuck this behind your stiff belt and keep it there until you turn it over to the night nurse when you do the narcotic count again. I know this is another 'first' for you, and so I'm sort of warning you. The head nurse always carries it in the daytime. You can get into real trouble if you misplace the key or if your count is incorrect." I slid the narcotic key holder inside my belt, next to my bandage scissors, and felt the tools of my trade pressing against my body. All during the evening they would be a constant reminder of the charge that was mine.

Continuing in a whisper Miss Donavan wanted to caution me more about Mr. Genoa. She took my arm firmly and steered me through the swinging metal door of the utility room. "One more thing. If something like that does happen on your shift—I mean if you have another Allen Street—remember you can call the Little Float. It's her duty to take care of all Allen Street discharges on the relief shift." (The Little Float was a nurse on special assignment who assisted with emergencies on the wards during the relief shift.) I nodded and couldn't think of anything to say.

"You do look worried, Miss Wright; let's go back into the medicine closet so we can talk and keep an eye on my patients. I haven't finished." Still wordless I followed her out the swinging door, unlocked the little room, and we stepped back in. Miss Donavan adjusted her cap again, and this time, not counting pills, she narrowed her eyes and looked straight into mine. I drew away to see her better, but the cupboard was in my way. Her eyes were nailing me to the cupboard doors. I could not move. "Now I was the Little Float once," she said, "and I had *seven* Allen Streets during that month. It was in the middle of the winter—lots of pneumonia. Seems all I did was go down the freight elevator with those people, their bodies, you know." She felt she had to explain. "That's what you use, you know, the freight elevator; that's the only one at that end of the tunnel that goes there. But the worst part was when I did the preparation, washing them, the bodily fluids, the eyes, the jaw, getting the mouth securely closed, and putting on the shroud—getting them ready to go."

My mouth was dry and the closet warm, Miss Donavan's eyes stayed fixed, and she kept talking. "You know, you can feel the spirit leave the body. If I didn't learn anything else when I was a student nurse in this hospital I learned that. I had a very dear patient once; I liked her a lot. Her name was Mary French. Everybody liked Miss French. She had congestive heart failure, and was here for a long time. And that's when I realized what I'm telling you. I was with her the very second that she died, and just like that," Miss Donavan snapped her fingers, "she wasn't here anymore. Her spirit wasn't here anymore, but I felt peaceful, and she looked peaceful, and I'll never forget that. I just went through the motions getting her body ready, and that's how it was, it was just her discarded body. Heavy, heavy legs, you know, because she had that edema. And when I pulled the shroud over her head and called the orderly to move her onto the gurney it all was just mechanical. That was my first time, and I'll tell you, it's a strange thing, and it's true—every time that happened, along with all the sadness there was peace—I can't explain it." She hesitated, "Well, that's what I wanted to tell you." Her eyes relaxed and I moved away from the cupboard as she smiled like an earnest school teacher who had just imparted a bit of wisdom to her student. I closed the door of the medicine cabinet and remembered only the sadness.

In my mind's eye I saw the water in the brook flowing toward the ocean. I thought of my father. He had lain in a great, long box next to our "library" table in the living room with flowers all about him. They had to lift me up to see him. He was quiet and peaceful but I felt only sadness.

I locked the medicine closet and secured the key holder inside my stiff belt while we walked toward the rows of patients. Miss Donavan said, "Anyway, call the Little Float if you need her for Mr. Genoa." And I knew my relief duty had started.

Everyone on the day shift had left when Miss Donavan put on her cape and said goodbye. All the curtains were drawn neatly to the wall, and every bed was visible from the Nurses' Station. White bedspreads were pulled taut with mitered corners even as the patients lay in assorted positions. The ward was more rectangular than square, with ten beds on each side and six at each end. A simple white table stood erect beside each bed with only a water glass on it, and at the end of every bed was a chair, precisely positioned, soldiers at attention. The quiet in the ward was a contrast from the activity of the day shift; only patients were present, the men in their blue johnnies lying against the white pillows, and they seemed peaceful. But I also sensed each one waiting and watching. Watching me, and waiting for me. I was the next act.

There is something comforting about specific tasks, like the routine of p.m. care for all patients, bringing a basin of water and a kidney basin for washing and teeth-brushing, taking temperatures, smoothing the rubber sheets and tightening the draw-sheets and giving every patient a back rub. This methodical activity carried me through the first hours as I rushed from patient to patient. The constant bedpan trips, carrying the oval-shaped stainless steel containers, covered with blue and white mattress-ticking covers, maybe one in each hand with a urinal hooked over one finger. I kicked open the utility room door and faced the huge copper hopper—a place to empty and flush—and along the wall the wooden racks to store pans and urinals. It was all my domain as I flushed and redistributed the receptacles, finally replacing them in orderly rows beside the over-sized toilet.

All during the late afternoon I felt the student, Mr. Smith, in bed 12, watching me race from patient to patient, in and out of curtained cubicles, to the utility room, back again, to the medicine closet, and to the center of the ward, to the Nurses' Station to check the treatment chart. Finally he called out to me, "Nurse, I wish I could help you. When they make me ambulatory I'll be happy to help you, Miss Wright." I accepted his offer almost as though he had asked me to dance, and I liked that he remembered my name from Miss Donavan's introduction. "I'd love it," I laughed. "We'll have fun doing this together!" The water basin I was carrying sloshed almost to spilling as I waltzed through the swinging door.

I told myself that I was getting there, doing just what Miss Donavan said, just keeping going. When I changed Mr. Genoa's bed after his inlaying catheter had become disconnected, I had felt his skin cooler, and just knowing that his fever was down, and hearing his quiet words, "Thank you, Nurse," had given me renewed energy.

"You're next," I said to Mr. Smith, who was smiling now as I pulled the curtains around his bed. "The water for your flaxseed poultice is about to boil so I need to change your dressing first."

The privacy of the curtains closed in on me and his disarming good looks caused me to fumble with the binder that held his dressing secure. As I removed the yellowish blood-stained gauze sponges from his infected sutures, my eyes followed the soft pattern of his hairy chest that tufted almost to his neck. And then, as though I expected it, I felt his hand on my breast; he had found me under my starched bib. I kept on with my work, replacing the soiled dressing with sterile sponges, taking my time, lingering in the sensation I was feeling in my body there in the cozy confines of the cubicle. "I've been watching you since you came on duty"; his voice was soft and clear and honest, and I smiled, a helpless half-smile, like I didn't know what to say. But the stirring deep inside of me held me there. I didn't even know this young man, I was in uniform, I was working, this was all out of line, it was all wrong, and yet I liked it.

I remembered Camp Jeffmore and thought about a late evening picnic—a weenie roast—Shy (the nickname for a boy named Harry) and I had been roasting hot dogs in the moonlight. The fire was warm and Shy wrapped his arm around me to hold my right breast. He was the first boy I had ever kissed. Back then it was the same vexation. I was regretful, I felt like I'd been weak, but inside I felt good. I knew these sensations were natural and yet I thought they must be denied or hidden. But this was beyond that; I was on duty, and it was totally unacceptable, totally inappropriate. My face burned.

I felt the roundness of the key holder pressed against my body along with the steel of my bandage scissors, and abruptly I pulled away from his caress, yanking the white curtains for the world to see me intact, in my starched apron and bib. "I'll bring you your flaxseed poultice," I said abruptly. And with the soiled dressing secure in the kidney basin I hastened toward the swinging door. I still had so much to do.

It was nearly ten o'clock and I knew the race was almost won. "You're doing great," I assured myself as I checked the treatment sheet. Four flaxseed poultices ordered for every four hours, and I needed to do them one more time. A symphony of snores rose softly in the dimmed ward, and except for an occasional cough a pervasive peacefulness enhanced my sense of accomplishment. I went into the utility room. I had been distracted when I made the last poultice, and had not had time to clean the black pot. (I would always feel guilty when I made a flaxseed poultice.) I needed to wash the pot before I could boil the water again. I was scrubbing vigorously when Miss Storey, the Relief Supervisor, stepped into my ward. She entered the bleak utility room with her black cape flying after her, her thin lips pressed together tightly until they burst open from the fury on her face. "Where have you been? Do you know that bed 6 has vomited all over his bed? Where have you been?"

Until then I had forgotten about the Relief Supervisor, but her sudden presence along with her outburst was like a shot, like I'd been attacked. I dropped my dirty pot into the sink and ran from her into the ward. I could think only of Allen Streets and Little Floats and rushed to Mr. Genoa's bed. He was snoring evenly.

"Over here, Miss Wright, over here," Miss Storey said, as she motioned to me with both hands, a scowl of disgust, a look of impatience on her face. "I said bed 6. Can't you hear?" It was Mr. Carter, a patient I had known on the day shift. "I'm sorry, Miss Wright, I'm really sorry; I didn't want to bother you," he said, as I rolled him over to pull away the soiled sheet. Miss Storey was scribbling notes on the white paper of her clipboard. After walking around the ward, stiff, unyielding, she left, her black cape still flapping, an image of a witch, I thought.

I moved on to Mr. Genoa's bed. His light was on. "It's the catheter; it's pulling, Nurse. Can you fix it?" I turned back his sheets to pull the catheter from under his hips and release his penis. He sighed, "Oh, thank you, Nurse, that's a relief"; and I heard the urine draining again into the glass jar hanging on one side of his bed. On the other side the suction pump made a rhythmic sound as it drained the part of him where his stomach had been removed.

I saved his flaxseed poultice for my last treatment of the night. "Here it is, Mr. Smith," I said. While holding his poultice aloft on a white enamel tray I drew back his top sheet. I acted like nothing had happened, but he said, "I'm sorry, Miss Wright," and raised up on his elbow, his eyes sparkling like sun on the water, "and I meant what I said—I'll help you when Dr. MacClaren lets me get up; you need help, you know, you can't just keep running." And I said, "This evening's running is almost over." I wondered if he could see through me, how I desired to flow with the water, rather than to dart back and forth to the water's edge, hesitant, fearful of getting into deeper water. "My name is Cliff," he said. "Please call me Cliff, and thanks for not getting mad at me." I pulled his sheet up under his chin like I was tucking in a child. "That's the way it is in this world," I said, nonchalant. "You have a good night, Cliff."

Feeling stupid and inadequate, I asked myself: What do I know about this world? I had left my desk next to Regina's, followed the brook to the creek, to the river, to reach the city by the ocean. I had felt free, in the flow of life. I thought the mysteries would be revealed to me by the outside world in a new place. Now I knew that my freedom came from my inside world. I knew I would never be a supervising nurse with a mean temperament. I had survived the first night of relief duty and all my men had survived too. I didn't care what Miss Storey had written on the white paper of her clipboard.

*Mary, Public Health Nurse in
North West End of Boston, 1943*

Home Delivery

It was after midnight when I received Tony Gallo's call.

"They're coming every ten minutes, Nurse; her pains are real bad, I think you'd better come." Tony and Angela Gallo had been instructed to call the delivery nurse and the Boston Lying In Hospital when the contractions became frequent and regular. Angela was scheduled to have her baby delivered at home. I was the delivery nurse on call, and had visited Angela regularly during her pregnancy.

"All right, Tony, I'm on my way," I responded. "Have you called the hospital? Are they sending a doctor?"

"Just talked to them. Yeah, the doctor's on his way too. We'll be waiting for you guys. I better go back to Angela now."

I heard the click and the change drop into the pay phone. I pulled my navy blue public health uniform over my head and checked the Gallo address again before calling the cab. During my six months on the Home Delivery service for the Community Health Association of Boston, I had attended the births of twenty-five babies at home in tenement buildings. My six-month assignment was ending. This would be my last delivery with a Harvard medical student in attendance.

I thrived on being in a place where I was really needed and every case was different. I never knew what to expect. There was always the possibility that the mother would be in labor all night and all the next day. Sometimes there were emergencies when we needed to call the ambulance to take our patient to the hospital. The medical student and I would stay with her until she delivered, no matter how long. Our patients were mothers who were poor, on relief. They delivered their babies without medication.

Mothers who could afford hospitalization experienced the modern methods, under the sedation of pain-deadening medication, a combination of morphine and scopolamine. They called it "twilight sleep." During their period of labor they thrashed about in beds protected by canvas side panels. The canvas covers were loosely tied in the center with soft ropes to prevent patients from falling out of bed. As the mother physically responded to pain, writhing in grotesque movements, she cried and called for help in an unintelligible voice. The nurses moved from bed to bed in the six-bed labor room, spreading patients' legs and checking for crowning, the appearance of a baby's head on the perineum. With fetus-scopes clamped on their heads and plugged into their ears, they leaned over the distended bodies to check the babies' hearts, placing the sensitive round instrument on the mother's abdomen as she heaved and sometimes thrust her legs out of the canvas tops, between the ropes. The drugged patients would not remember; only the nurses in the labor room remembered.

In contrast to hospital deliveries in the forties, mothers gave birth in the tenements naturally. There were no barriers, no buffers; it was stark reality, the hot water and the cockroaches, the pain and the joy. Harvard's third-year medical students were the "doctors" in the tenements. They had completed their courses in obstetrics, and had attended deliveries in the Boston Lying In Hospital, under supervision of resident obstetricians. It was 1942, during World War II, and the majority of medical students were Army or Navy cadets. Their uniforms further enhanced their image: "A nice Navy doctor delivered my baby," a tenement mother would boast.

The students' obstetric assignment lasted only three weeks so they were fortunate to experience even one home delivery. Some of the young men were poised, impersonal, almost haughty. Others were friendly, vaguely appreciative of my help, but tiresome in their effort to appear experienced. On the other hand, as the delivery nurse, I had confidence in my professional skills but felt shy and inadequate with men in general.

The previous week I had attended a home delivery with Lynch O'Leary, a med student from Virginia. "I've chosen this field," he said, "decided I want to take care of the women." We were delivering the baby of Nick and Filamena Ballerina in the North End.

"Nurse," Lynch ordered me, "boil the instruments now!"

I had already sterilized them.

"They are ready, Doctor," I said.

He didn't call Filamena by name. He called her "Mother." I knew he was a doctor who called all his obstetric patients "Mother."

Filamena had delivered quickly. It was her eighth baby, and all the children had been herded into the flat upstairs during her labor. Nick, the father, sat in a straight wooden chair in the corner, watching and wordless, while he opened and closed his pocket knife. But when his baby boy was born he became friendly, brandishing with pride his slim green bottle of anisette. "My brothers and I, we make this," he said. "You must drink to my son!" He and Lynch, arms around each other, raised their glasses and toasted the baby several times. It was three o'clock in the morning as we sipped the cordial and nibbled on biscotti. We celebrated Italian style in the tenement across the street from the Old North Church. I had become accustomed to the liqueur with its licorice-like flavor because routinely we accepted; if we didn't accept the Sicilian hospitality they were insulted. The first time I had refused, saying I couldn't drink it on an empty stomach. They insisted on making a two-inch-high salami sandwich and stood by to watch me eat it so I could drink a toast with them.

After that birth in the North West End, Lynch gave me a ride home from the Ballerinas, and when I unlocked my door he followed me into my apartment. He slipped off his Army jacket and threw it on the arm of the sofa in our living room as though he had been invited to stay.

"Why did you do that?" I asked. "You're on your way home."

"C'mon," he said, helping me take off my coat. "We worked too hard tonight. We deserve a little fun." Lynch had been sure of himself during the delivery, in charge, giving orders. I felt his arms around me, strong, vice-like—not hugs. He tried to kiss me.

I was still thinking of Filamena's baby boy, snuggled against her chest. I wriggled my hands free and shoved him away. "It's late," I said. "You must go home."

"Say, are you some kind of prude? Look, I'm in the Army already. We don't know what to expect tomorrow or the next day. Might as well live it up." I felt the length of his body pressing against mine, and we dropped together onto the sofa. I struggled to get up, and as I turned my head, the brass buttons of his uniform jacket dug into my scalp. The sofa was small and Lynch slid away from me.

I stood up, smoothed out my uniform skirt, and said, as he lay sprawled on the floor, "You'd better go now. This's one place where you don't give orders!"

He got up slowly and sat on the sofa, hunched over with his head in his hands. "Say, you really are something. Guess I'd better go."

When I lowered the blinds in my bedroom, the morning was awakening, the darkness turning blue-gray, and I would sleep. There was the possibility that I would be called again before my roommate took over the duty. Another delivery nurse and I shared the two-bedroom apartment on the "wrong" side of Beacon Hill, and we took turns being on call for deliveries.

❧

Incredible freedom buoyed our spirits as we lived our lives for the first time, free from authority and the restrictions of nurses' residences. Yet we felt the nearly overwhelming responsibility of bringing babies into the world in the most meager circumstances, into a world raging with war.

To some extent I was worldly. After all, I was twenty-one years old. I had grown up in a small town, and now in a big city brought new lives into a frantic world. I had attended many deaths in the hospital; how many I didn't know because I'd never counted them. But

I had counted the births I had attended, twenty-five, either in the tenements of Boston or at the Boston Lying In Hospital.

However, my worldliness was lacking when it came to men. In the hospital, I learned about the anatomy and physiology and biology of men. I learned about men's bodies. I took care of men, washed them inside and out, held their urinals and their penises, adjusted their catheters. Yet personally, although my thoughts were laced with desire and fantasies, my naivety was an embarrassment for me. During my first year in nurses' training, Edith Edgewood asked me to go on a blind date. She was older than I, seemed quiet and demure, had graduated from college before nurses' training. "He's really cute," she said. "He's studying engineering at Northeastern." I felt flattered when she chose me. We met her boyfriend and my blind date, John, at a brownstone house on Beacon Street near the esplanade. They offered us drinks, and I accepted as though I knew what I was drinking. But when I tasted the icy drink and realized it was alcohol, I didn't react, I just pretended to drink it. This was an experience I wanted to be part of, to be in the swim of fun, to become sophisticated and knowledgeable and comfortable with a man who would care about me, someone I would care about too. I felt carefree, but at the same time insecure when I was introduced to John. He was tall and neat, his hair slick and freshly combed, and his smile friendly as he looked at me, his eyes roving, evaluating. "I like your beer jacket," he said. I was wearing my roommate's tan safari jacket. She had bought it on sale at Bonwit Tellers on Copley Square. I had never heard it called a "beer jacket." "That'd be good to wear at Jake Wirth's," he said as he lifted his glass and urged me to drink. "We'll have to go there sometime."

Edith suddenly disappeared with her boyfriend into another room. John sat down on the couch and playfully pulled me down beside him. "Now, isn't this cozy?" he said, and reached over me to pull the tiny chain that turned off the lamp on a circular table. I was uncomfortable in the darkness and heard John squirming around. In that moment I realized that he had put me in a certain category, the stereotype that nurses are "fast," nurses know everything, present a nurse with an erect penis and she'll take care of it. A narrow beam of light shone through the triangular leaded glass window in the front door. When I saw the whiteness standing forth and the fallen trousers and the blackness of the shades pulled down and heard the giggling in the next room, I left. I opened the front door and ran out to the glimmer of the park lights along the Charles River. People sauntered past me, and I hurried down the esplanade until I came to the boat house. I sat alone on a park bench, listening to the river water slap against the sides of the small sailboats. I felt in unison with them, tossed back and forth by the current. I was consumed with my own sense of power, yet felt ambivalent about my actions. I so wanted to love and be loved. I walked back to my dorm on Charles Street.

❦

That was two years ago. Now I was a delivery nurse but I still had little experience with men. When Tony Gallo's call came in the middle of the night to tell me his wife was in labor, I felt cold, and I shivered as I dressed, not knowing what was going to happen, how the delivery would go. Another part of me was wondering who the med student would be. Had he delivered a baby? Would I have to do it myself? What would he be like? Would I like him? Would he like me?

I was wide awake when I ran down the brick walkway through the iron gates to the taxicab parked by the curb, its lights flashing. Geno, the cabby at the Charles River taxi stand, knew about these calls and he knew the city. He knew Scollay Square and the North West End, the South End, and East Boston. He sat in his taxi like he was a part of it. I climbed in the back seat and drew my black bag in beside me, holding it firmly as Geno lifted the flag on his meter to start it ticking. He shifted gears, and his taxi swung away from the curb.

"Where to this time?" Geno asked, twisting his head around to look at me.

"Two-forty Paris Street in East Boston," I said, and relaxed into the seat, still holding the handles of my bag. "I'm sure glad you know your way around, Geno." I breathed the stale air in his cab, the exhaled odor of alcohol and tobacco of former occupants, and I felt a comforting familiarity.

Geno's cab, loose at the joints, swerved and careened through the haphazard network of one-way streets and tunnels with a sureness that gave me an inner sense of order. He knew the urgency. Sometimes urgency piled on top of urgency when the city practiced a blackout. All of life seemed deadly serious with the terrifying news of war. Geno and I in the heavy silence of his cab shared a common commitment, to do whatever was at hand for us to do. He would get me there. I would be there for the baby to be born. We were part of the uncertainty of the whole world, and yet our task for the moment was clear.

Emerging from the tunnel under the Charles River, Geno steered his cab through the narrow, uneven streets until suddenly we were between rows of grayed buildings, grayer at night, stark and leaning together, like an abandoned burned forest. My frivolous fantasy, a serious, friendly medical student, darted in and out of my mind, and I liked being teased by the possibility.

"There's a light up there, must be the place. Yeah, that's it. I'll go up with you, Nurse."

The beam from Geno's flashlight found the stairway as I hurried over the stoop and up the worn, slanted wooden steps, creaking and shifting with our weight, to the third floor where we had seen the light. We followed the shaft of light down the hallway, past an open toilet closet. "Man, that's some stink," said Geno.

Tony, Angela's husband, stood in the doorway. He was a short, sturdy man, his teeth white in his smile on a dark unshaven face. "You came quick," he said. He took my black bag from Geno. "What a pretty nurse; boy, is Angel gonna be glad to see you!"

I had been in Angela's flat before, providing prenatal care and preparing her for the home delivery. In the daytime I had come on the subway, the El, and walked down the treeless street. Although it was depressing, there was an air of comradery among the people who greeted me along the way. Everything seemed more dismal at night; the meager flat was a kitchen with two bedrooms, each opening at opposite ends of the kitchen. One door was closed. Angela came out of the open door. She was cradling her bulging body, her hands clasped together low, as though she were already holding her baby. I saw the rise, the tightening, as her robe drew taut. "I'm getting one, Nurse; they're comin' fast, Nurse." I reached under her robe to feel her abdomen, checked my watch, and started timing the contraction.

"Where are all the kids, Tony?" I asked.

"They's asleep. Take a look. Isn't that something? Like a pile of pillows, all them little kids! They'll sleep right through. Least I hope they do." He held open the door to the other room. Little Tony and his three sisters were asleep on one bed. The door did not latch. Tony replaced the rough chunk of concrete to hold it closed, and lifted the coffee pot from the stove.

"Cup of coffee 'fore you go?" he asked Geno. Geno pulled his frayed yellow and black visor down on his forehead. "No, thanks a lot, but we're short-handed tonight. I better get going. Good luck to you guys. See you later, Nurse." He touched his hand to his cap, a little salute. I heard the stairs creak loudly, two steps at a time; he hadn't lost his momentum.

"Help me go pee, Tony." Angela's hair was pulled back in a knot, yet dark damp curls framed her face. She had abandoned all thoughts of how she looked. She smiled weakly, displaying teeth with brown spots of decay. "Just feel like I gotta go all the time, Nurse; do you think it'll be soon?"

"You just went, Angel," Tony said, "but it's O.K., you can do anything you want; come on, let's go again." I watched as Tony gathered all of Angela into his arms and guided her across the dark hallway to the closet. Angela rested on the toilet, her pink chenille robe soaking up the moisture on the floor. As she lifted herself up and regained her balance, she said, "I feel the baby is really low." She shuffled back to the bedroom between Tony and me. We would not have much time.

Back in the bedroom I removed Angela's soiled robe while she hoisted herself onto the bed. "Yes, the baby has dropped way down," I said, feeling the head well engaged in the pelvis as I examined her.

"They're all here, Nurse, all them newspaper pads you had me sew. I got big ones, and them littler ones," Angela said as she pointed to the corner of the room.

I nodded, and said, "That's great, Angela; you did everything on the list." They were neatly stacked, newspaper pads, made of several layers of newspaper and covered with old sheets, sewn together with heavy white thread. I placed a large pad under Angela, and another near the edge of the bed where the baby would be born. Overhead a bright light bulb hung from an electric cord anchored to the ceiling.

"We're almost set; the doctor should be here any minute. He had further to go," I said. "Hope he didn't get lost."

I had been alone before when the baby came. I hoped this wouldn't happen now, but I wasn't uneasy. I was amused at myself because I was more concerned about what he would be like than whether he came on time. I removed the small metal basin from my bag and checked the instruments, two clamps and one pair of sharp scissors. "Let's boil these right now, Tony." I placed the sterile cord dressing on the table near the bed, and the preparation for the delivery was complete. I was expecting the medical student almost as though he were a guest who was late. The party might go on without him.

I slipped on my white apron and tied it behind me and, fluffing up my hair for a fleeting moment, I wondered how I looked. Did I look like I had been awakened out of a sound sleep? I scrubbed my hands in the cold water running from the high rusty faucet of the kitchen sink. The water gurgled loudly as it emptied through the metal pipe exiting through a hole cut in the wooden floor. A blackened kettle of water was steaming on the back burner of the spindly kerosene stove. On the other back burner stood a tall, gray, cracked enamel coffee pot, also steaming. "Lots of hot water and lots of coffee; that's the least I can do!" Tony was punching the second hole in a small can of Pet milk with a can opener. "Do you like milk in your coffee, Nurse? You better have a cup of coffee. Don't you think that doc oughta be here by now? That lady at the hospital told me he was on his way."

Angela called from her bed, "Here comes another; God, Tony, help me, help me now!" Tony and I rushed to hold her hands. We had turned off the light after each contraction so she could relax. When the light came back on several cockroaches scurried away to darkness. Angela clung to us as we watched the rush of water splashing onto the wood floor. "My water broke, didn't it, Nurse? My water broke!"

There was a knock on the door, and at the same time I heard it open. The medical student appeared at the bedroom door. Dressed in a Navy cadet uniform, he looked like he was late for his ship. His flashlight was still shining, and he was shining, too, from the 200-watt bulb over Angela's bed reflecting the moisture on his face.

"Oh, I'm sorry," he said, as he ran his hand over his short crew cut and flicked off his flashlight.

He looked down at Angela, lying crosswise on the bed. "I heard you when I came down the hall. Heard you say your water broke. God, I'm sorry I didn't get here sooner. I got lost. I don't know my way around this part of town."

He was appraising me as well as the whole scene, I thought, as he looked around the room and back at me. I placed my hand on Angela's abdomen and looked at my watch to time a contraction that was beginning.

"My name's Bill, Bill Harris, and I want you to give me direction, just tell me what I need to do. I'm really sorry I'm late."

Again he looked blankly around the flat. "Where can I hang this?" he asked as he removed his Navy uniform jacket. Holding his jacket in one hand he walked to the bedside where I sat beside Angela, and he placed his other hand on my hand as I felt her hardened abdomen. "Say, I'm sure glad you're here; looks like you have everything all set. That's what I was told. That you girls are great—not to worry—the delivery nurse will be there." He removed his hand from mine and looked around for a place to hang his jacket.

I liked his directness, his clean good looks, and the way his hair, even though clipped short, seemed to be straining to curl. "Hang your jacket on that hanger over the open door, Bill," I said, as I smoothed my white apron over my hips and lifted the fetus-scope away from my ears. He slid his jacket over the hanger and placed it within the door frame next to my navy blue raincoat.

"I'm Mary, Bill, and this is Angela; she's as courageous as they come. Yes, you heard right; her membrane ruptured just as you came down the hall." He looked worried. I put my hand on his arm and reassured him, "Everything's going to be all right."

"Thanks," he said, and I heard him take a deep breath.

"It doesn't matter that you just got here. But Angela is almost ready to deliver. You better start scrubbing your hands," I said, and walked with him to the kitchen sink. "We have only cold water, but Tony will pour some hot from the kettle after our first scrub."

Tony was smiling, relaxed now, holding out his hand to Bill. "I'm Tony, Doc; sure glad you made it—you a Navy doctor? I saw that brass on your uniform."

Bill shook his hand. "Well, I guess you'd say I'm a Navy doctor. Yes, I'm a Navy cadet now while I'm in medical school, and I'm the doctor while I'm here." He shrugged his shoulders like it really didn't matter. I liked his answer. After all, it seemed as though everyone was either in the Army or Navy or Marines or planning to be there soon. Or they were riveters, like Tony hoped to be. He was still on relief, but went every morning down to the hall for possible employment at the shipyards; for the first time in years he had a chance for a job.

Bill wrapped his rubber apron around his khaki shirt and pants, and I reached up to straighten the loop around his neck and then tied it behind him. I liked the feeling of dressing his tall lean body. He laughed and said, "This is some slicker they provide for us," as he smoothed the dark gray shiny apron over his thighs and stepped to the sink to scrub his hands.

Tony held the coffee pot in one hand and the Pet milk can in the other. "How about it, Doc? Do you want milk in your coffee?"

"No thanks, no thanks a lot. I don't use milk; in fact, let's save the coffee for later," he told Tony.

I was checking the fetal heart. Angela drew her hand over her forehead and took a deep breath. She clutched and pulled on the towels I had anchored on the other side of the bed for her to hang onto in order to bear down. "This's the last one, Tony, I mean the *last one*. No more babies. You're gonna have to stay away from me forever. Oh, God, here it comes again; hang onto me, Tony."

"It's most over, Angel; we done this a lot and you're doing good again."

Bill whispered to me, "What is that? Is she crowning already?"

His gloved hand was held motionless in the air, waiting for something to happen. He could not hide his inexperience. His unabashed honesty, his eagerness to understand, and his willingness to flow with the new experience aroused my respect.

"Yes, that's the head, the baby's head. It's coming, so get ready with both hands." My gloved hands were ready to guide the baby's head when it appeared.

"Will you keep your hands here too? I need to be sure I'm doing this O.K." He placed his hands just inside of mine, cupped in mine.

"All right, Angela, take another deep breath; you're doing fine," I said. "One or two more like that and your baby will be here." Bill and I sat on two stools at the edge of the bed, a large gray basin in front of our splattered shoes.

Bill whispered again, "You really think it will come with the next push?" I felt his shoulder next to mine.

"Yes, just get in the rhythm of it like Angela, go with her as she pushes; you'll feel the baby's head coming, almost, almost, and then finally and you will be ready. O.K., now you see her contraction; here it comes."

Angela's hands were white as she clenched the towel in one hand and Tony's hand in the other. The baby's head came out, face down, into Bill's hands, my hands just underneath his, guiding, securing. "That's it, that's it, slow now, feel around the neck; is there a cord there?" Bill's fingers felt gingerly. "No cord, it's all clear." I breathed freely again and said, "Good, good, and now you can push some more, Angela, and your baby will be here." And the baby was born.

Bill slid his fingers around the ankles of the tiny slippery baby and held her up so that Angela could see. He cautiously patted the baby on the back. She sputtered and cried and he said, "Angela, Tony, you have a little girl!"

Angela was sitting up in bed. Tony drew a broad black comb through her hair and handed her two bobby pins so that she could fasten her damp curls behind her ears. She liked her coffee strong and Tony brought it to her with hard thin cookies. She dunked them and laughed, and in a quiet shy voice she said, as she looked at her baby in her lap, "She's really pretty, isn't she?"

"All my girls are pretty, Angel, but you're the prettiest of them all," said Tony. His cheeks were glistening; his eyes flooded with tears. "I'm so happy you're all right, Angel."

I felt a cluster of bedbugs hugging the bottom of the mattress as I tucked in the clean sheet. I pulled my hand away; I recognized the tiny bulges that seemed glued to where they lived. "Not until they tear down the whole row of them dumps will we get rid of the bedbugs and roaches," the Board of Health man told me when I reported the infestation months ago.

"Mary—Mary—that's what her name is. We're naming her after you, Nurse. If she'd been a boy we'd have named him Bill."

We walked through the iron gateway, and up the brick walk of Primus Avenue. It was early morning and Bill had driven me home.

We stopped at the steps in front of my apartment and after he hugged me he stood back, holding his hands on my shoulders. "You were great, really great, thanks a lot."

"Well, thanks," I said, reaching up to hold his hands, "and wasn't Angela great?"

"Let's talk about you, Mary. I want to see you again," he said. "This's my last day on OBS. Thank God, that's one specialty I won't choose."

"You don't have to decide that right now," I said.

"Oh, I know," he said, "but I'm pretty sure it'll be cardiology, once I get this Navy thing over. But the question I have right now is if you'll see me again?"

"Probably not, Bill, at least not in the near future," I said, and explained that I had to report to Fort Devens after a vacation in my home in Pennsylvania. "I joined the Army Nurse Corps and I'm waiting for my orders."

My apartment was on Primus Avenue. Not really an avenue or even a street, it was more like a courtyard leading to the front door of the shingled two-story apartment building. Bill led me away from the steps to the rusty wrought iron settee that sat neglected in the shrubbery in the corner of the courtyard. We talked about ourselves. His home was in Maine with his mother and sister; his father had died in a boating accident when he was eight years old. Bill had gone to Yale before medical school. He liked to ice skate and he had been an opera lover since his mother started taking him when he was nine years old.

I liked his kisses, and when we said good night in a tender and passionate embrace, I was so relaxed I almost abandoned myself. Too bad, I thought, and here I have given myself to the Army. He invited me to go home with him at Christmastime and meet his family, and I accepted. He seemed weary but alert in his Navy uniform as he adjusted his visored hat and with a slight salute, he said, "I'm at your service; I'll come over here to your place and cook dinner for you tomorrow night if that's O.K. And I'll bring the food, pork and applesauce, because that's what I fix the best." I responded that it sounded like a good idea. "So I'll see you then; six o'clock is fine," I said, and closed the door behind me.

It was four o'clock in the morning, and I stood in the bathtub and undressed, just in case I had brought a bedbug home from the Gallos. And as I slid between my sheets my weariness gave way to a peacefulness that was more than the happiness about the Gallo's baby; it was a kind of reassurance about myself.

I arrived early at the depot the day I was to report for duty in the Army Nurse Corps. Early enough to have a cup of coffee before I boarded the bus. It was a new beginning, a fresh awareness. Was I letting go of my feeling of inadequacy about men? If so, the timing was right because I was joining a men's army. I thought of the morning Mary Gallo was born; I had met a special man, a man whose life was not centered on himself, a very kind man, Tony Gallo. The extraordinary perfume of the love of a man for his wife as she gave birth had lingered in the flat at 240 Paris Street.

And how about Bill? Would he be in my life? After these last few weeks of getting to know each other, and visiting with his family, I embraced the possibility. We would be writing many letters. Uncertainty coupled with hope flooded over me; we were all caught up in the current of reality: our country was at war. I clutched the manila envelope that contained my orders. I must go with the river. In the Army I would have no control of where I was going or whom I would be with.

Several months later Bill's censored letters suddenly stopped coming. I received word from his mother that he was missing in action; the ship on which he had been stationed had been torpedoed and sunk.

Lieutenant Mary Alberta Wright,
Army Nurse Corps, 1944-1946

Mary and Norm on their wedding day, February 10, 1947

Go with the River

We were going to move again, this time to Los Angeles. My husband, Norm, had accepted a job as the national sales manager of a major chemical corporation. It was now October of 1960. Two years earlier, when our youngest son, John, was six weeks old, we had moved with our five children from Menlo Park, California to Upper Saint Clair, a suburb of Pittsburgh, Pennsylvania. Norm worked for Kaiser Corporation and had been promoted to manager of industrial chemicals for the eastern division of the company, but he never stopped searching for a better position. We were on the fast track. "I need to make up for all the time I lost in the Army," Norm said. Our life in the East had settled into a comfortable routine, and when he accepted this new job, part of me said, "Slow down—," but I knew I had to start packing.

Ever since Norm had been wounded in the Battle of the Bulge during World War II he had been anxious to get his life on the move again. He had spent two years in the infantry and then two years in Army hospitals for reconstructive surgery to repair his left leg, which had been shattered by a German carbine.

Norm was a native San Franciscan, and it had been quite a concession for him to be willing to live in the East. But I was a Pennsylvanian and enjoyed coming back to the familiar Allegheny forest land where my family could visit us and get to know Norm and our children. I knew we would someday fly back to the West, and that was all right because I was a converted Californian.

We had talked a lot about the pros and cons of living in the East versus the West. In Pennsylvania a friendly woods bordered our two-acre lot and a stream filled the lake at the bottom of the hill. The boys skied down the hill in the winter and in the springtime they caught a fish before breakfast to take to school in a glass jar for science class. But the ready access of forest and stream in the East lost to the weather and charm of life in the West; we welcomed this new opportunity, and the chance to go home to California where we had spent the first thirteen years of our marriage.

I had met Norm at Stanford University; we both had returned to school on the G.I. Bill. I had served two years in the Army Nurse Corps. It had been easy for me to hop on Norm's fast train; we were caught up in the freedom of being out of the service. We spent Sundays in San Francisco, a dazzling jewel of a city. "Come on, I'll show you Ocean Beach." Norm's enthusiasm for the city he had grown up in created a mutual intoxication. In the cold and the sunshine, with the sound of the surf, I became addicted to enchiladas smothered with onions, to the atmosphere of a carnival on the beach.

We climbed the stairs to the Legion of Honor and sat for hours on the steps, not feeling the chilly concrete, while we fell in love in the fall of 1946. We walked through Norm's old neighborhood, down Lake Street, almost like a street in my home town of Warren, Pennsylvania, with the burnished leaves from autumn trees scattered along our way. As we talked, we roamed among our childhood days, sharing our deepest thoughts and secrets. We were married three months after we met, February 10, 1947.

I have often described our last ten years on the San Francisco Peninsula as "our ten-year production period" because our daughter and four sons were born during this time. Norm earned his degrees in engineering and business and began working in San Francisco and Oakland. I dropped out of Stanford and became a full-time mother and housewife. Like many postwar families, we were able to purchase a home with no down payment because of our veteran status.

Now in 1960 we were planning to move back to California, to Los Angeles. The country was tuned in at night to the Kennedy/Nixon debates. The Pittsburgh Pirates had won the pennant, and our two oldest sons, Normie, age twelve, and Peter, age eight, were caught up in their own baseball victories. Our daughter, Mary, was six, and she was reluctant to leave her best friend, Molly

Yingling, whose father had built the finest playhouse right next door; the girls were inseparable. Our two youngest sons, four-year-old George and two-year-old John, more than anyone, looked forward to getting on a plane again.

Climbing the back steps after raking the leaves in our Pennsylvania yard, Norm commented, "I have really liked living in the East. I think the tougher schools, the tradition, and also the structure necessary with the cold weather have been a good thing for this family."

"I won't miss the snow suits," I said, remembering the first time I bundled George up and placed him outside in the front yard to help his brothers and sister build a snowman. After a few minutes he rang the doorbell. "It hurts," he said. During two years those snow suits had been on and off a million times, or at least it seemed that way.

Packing and moving was at the top of my list for disliked tasks. Packing and moving while my husband was flying around the country on business trips was an even more deplorable job. Norm started his job on the first of October and commuted to and from Los Angeles. His trips home to Pittsburgh were less and less frequent. Thanksgiving was coming and Norm called, "Let's just let the realtor handle the sale of our house and you and the gobbies (his affectionate reference to our children) can fly to L.A. on the day before Thanksgiving."

I had been packing for weeks, and now I knew I faced almost total exhaustion as I organized everything for the move. I had long ago adopted my mother's motto,

"Go with the river." But this time I wanted to push the river. After the moving van pulled away from our empty house on Gunston Hall Drive, my friend and neighbor, Gayle Hall, herded us into her station wagon and delivered us to the nearest motel.

The Beale Motel on Route 19 appeared almost desolate, located in a large field near the highway with tall grasses covering its foundation. The children, weary with sadness about leaving their friends, yet excited about the flight the next morning, were sprawled on the beds of our two connecting rooms. My thoughts consumed me; I did not hear the children until they were asleep, the ebb and flow of their quiet breathing. I could not sleep, yet I was dreaming, dreaming of endings, doors closing, boxes sealed tight, rugs rolled away leaving bare floors. Keys, no longer needed, were hunched together on the bedside table. Emptiness was filled by a cricket's song—crickets in November. One cricket kept me awake yet dreaming all night. I searched for him but could not find him. He was safe in a space beneath the uneven wooden floors, with tongue and groove mismatched. I waited for morning.

Gayle drove us to the airport at dawn, her station wagon bulging with children and baggage. Twelve-year-old Normie was finally caught up in the excitement of our trip, but at the same time he was holding two-year-old Johnnie. I didn't know what I would do without him. He was a perfectionist like his father; he had developed a habit of attending to details. He kept reminding me of the essential steps to accomplish this undertaking. "Where are the tickets? What is the flight number? Are all the suitcases labeled?" I thought that surely he must tire of his father's constant order, "Remember to help your mother." As if he could ever forget.

The plane rocked and rolled, and suddenly fell as if to drop out of the sky. We strained against our seat belts as a thunder storm and uneven air flow rocked the plane, causing it to fall periodically deep distances in the darkness of the sky. Finally the great turboprop plane broke through the storm, but the bumpiness continued. George asked Peter and Normie why they had the yellow (air sickness) bags pressed to their faces. As the flight became smoother Mary helped the stewardesses dispatch drinks to the passengers; they staggered back and forth between the rows of seats with trays dripping. I could hardly wait for the flight to end in Los Angeles. Norm would meet us at the airport. The plane landed with a series of thumps, bounced up and down on the runway, and finally rolled toward the blinking lights of the terminal.

I saw him first. As always my heart skipped its beats. I thought he looked tired, but then he was jubilant, his marvelous smile flashing and showing his even white teeth. Norm was hurrying past the others to get to us. The children had practiced "California, here we come, right back where we started from—." Norm hugged me as I held John, and standing amidst the huddle that was our family I sank deeply into the strength of his hard strong body. And he said to me, "My God, you're so comfortable; we're all so lucky."

We drove to the Ambassador Hotel where we would stay for ten days until our furniture arrived. Norm said, "What a Thanksgiving! After dinner I'll show you the house I rented in Palos Verdes. You'll love the area. It's the best place to live in L.A." He was thinking of the sun-drenched weekends when we could go to the beach, and play tennis. He was proud of Normie's athletic skill and his winning at tennis tournaments in Pittsburgh. Those ten days at the Ambassador were like a vacation, yet the children's boisterous activity in our suite of rooms and other parts of the sprawling hotel created a challenge for me in terms of keeping some sense of order.

Finally the moving van arrived, and we became casually but adequately settled in our house at 4116 Via Picaposte. It was in the wooded section, with an abundance of fragrant blossoms, and in December a welcome change from the chilling rain and snow we had left in the East. Just over the hill was the ocean.

We had less than a week to get ready for Christmas, but first I needed to enroll the older children in their schools. Peter and Mary would be in the elementary school nearby, and Normie would travel farther by bus to Rolling Hills Junior High School. Everyone had missed time in school; I wanted to get them started as soon as possible. It was good to be back with some structure and purpose to my day. I felt unsettled; Norm sensed my dissonance.

"Remember, this is temporary," he said. "As soon as we sell our house we'll buy a new one here. I've already got a realtor looking for us."

I took a deep breath and said to myself, "Go with the river, Mary; even going over the rapids can be fun!"

Norm had one more meeting in San Francisco before Christmas. "It's the last trip this year," he announced as he tossed his briefcase into his car and drove away to the L.A. airport. He called early that evening from San Francisco. "Gosh, honey, a strange thing just happened to me." His voice quivered as he continued talking. "It really scared me." I held the telephone receiver tight against my ear as though to steady myself. I waited for him to speak again. "I called you because I need to know that I'm O.K. Darling, did I ever tell you how special you are?"

"Yes, yes," I said, "but what's the matter? Where are you?"

"Nothing's the matter, I guess. But I had to call you. You know, somehow you make things seem O.K."

"But what's happened? Where are you?" I asked.

His voice was still anxious. "I just left Mama's house and thought I'd walk around the old neighborhood before I drive to the airport. Then all of a sudden I wasn't in my body. I can't explain it. God, it was weird. But I managed to walk over to this phone booth on Clement Street. I hardly remember getting here. Now I think I'm all right. Do I sound O.K. to you?"

"Well, yes," I said, "but what you're saying doesn't sound right. Were you feeling O.K. at Mama's?"

"Oh, yes, and we ate at Grisson's. Something told me to take Mama out to dinner tonight. Now I'm on my way home."

I heard his breathing into the telephone, and then he laughed and said, "Say, this's a funny thing. I can see my reflection in the window of this phone booth but I don't feel that I'm here."

A heaviness rolled into my body, beginning in my stomach, invading my chest, and spreading throughout my entire being. I was speechless. I struggled to respond, remembering how tired he had looked at the airport the day we arrived in L.A. "Sweetheart," I said, "you're really very tired; maybe you should spend the night at Mama's."

"Oh, no," he said, "I just need to get home. Maybe I shouldn't have stayed over to take Mama out but I'm glad I did. So now I'm on my way. I'll see you in a few hours. Do you hear me?"

"Yes," I said, "I hear you, honey. I'll be waiting for you."

It was midnight when he arrived home. "Sorry I worried you," Norm said, as he laid his hat on the foot locker in the entry hall, "but I felt unreal in that phone booth—didn't even recognize my own hat. Now that I'm home I'm O.K."

Bed and each other never felt so good. We promised ourselves a completely relaxed Christmas holiday, but

Christmas was more bustle than ever. The children were getting bigger, and the toys were getting bigger. Many gifts needed to be assembled: a basketball hoop to be attached to the garage, a backyard tent, and a gasoline filling station. Our house was smaller than the one we had left, and we were resigned to a smaller tree, but then it seemed brighter as it was loaded with so many lights. Norm put on a record he had brought me: Steve Allen's "This Could Be the Beginning of Something Big."

Christmas Day was over. Normie dribbled the basketball and executed his slam dunk before calling it quits. George and John were already tucked in bed, exhausted. Peter and Mary were putting away their bikes. Finally Norm and I sat with our glasses of sherry, weary and happy, as we turned out the lights on another Christmas.

The morning after Christmas, as I lay in the warmth of Norm's arm, my face brushing against his unshaven chin, we marveled that we were finally getting things together again in California. We could hear Normie and Peter in the kitchen getting their breakfast. "No, you don't. I'm first," Normie shouted as they went crashing out the side door to the driveway and the basketball hoop. We heard the ball bounce off the hoop amidst scuffling and laughter. Mary and George were already in the tent in the backyard.

"The big boys have got to start being nicer to their sister," Norm announced. "I don't like the way they tease her."

And then Johnnie wandered into our room and came over to our bed. He had climbed out of his crib, his blond hair sticking up in all directions, nose running and his "nighty-nights" looking excessively soggy. "Now that one's yours," Norm joked, and a moment later I thought he was laughing. I was laughing and reaching for Johnnie when I turned and realized Norm was not laughing. He was gasping for breath, his left arm had become rigid, and suddenly his entire body seemed consumed in spasm. I screamed for Normie. I pounded Norm's chest and breathed into his mouth. The boys rushed in, looking terrified, and I shouted, "Go next door and get Mr. Good; Daddy needs a doctor!" The heavy feeling that I had had that evening when Norm called me from San Francisco spread throughout my shaking body. "Darling, Daddy, my God, we love you, come back, come back," I sobbed, feeling him slide away, wanting my breath to become his breath, but I was losing him; I was desperately helpless and alone.

Sirens in the distance became louder, closer, and I knew already it would be too late. As the bluish color filled his face and chest I felt Norm leave the room and part of me went with him.

Suddenly our bedroom was full of people. Edna Good, my next door neighbor, took me by the arm and moved me away from the bedside so that the ambulance men could do their job. The firemen pulled in equipment. Someone took me to the kitchen where the children waited. Normie stood by me as I sank into a chair, his arm around me. I was covered with little hands and the warmth of little bodies. We were all crying except for Normie, who I'll always remember tried so hard even then to be strong. Moments later a man in a white jacket came to the kitchen door. "Mrs. Shaw," he said, "your husband is dead."

"I know," I said, and sat quietly, holding our children, and I heard my voice, saying a prayer for strength. I do not recall the next hours very clearly. Neighbors helped me to make telephone calls to our families, and I called Cliff Smith, the minister in Mt. Lebanon, Pennsylvania who had been our Sunday School teacher and a dear friend. I was aware of the executive vice president of Norm's company, who drew Normie aside to tell him that he was now the "man of the family." "Take your hands out of your pockets," he said to Normie, and slapped his back as though to make him stand straighter. I wanted him to leave our house. I was numb.

The next few days were suffocating. There was the terrible man in the funeral home, with his vacant, sugary words. "You want the very best for your loved one, I'm sure," he said, as he escorted me through the rows of satin-lined coffins. My brother, Tom, was with me. Suddenly I bolted out of the incense-filled room, clutching Tom's arm as we escaped into the street. "I'll take care of it," Tom said. "You don't have to go in there again." We were both strangers in Los Angeles, two lost souls trying to make funeral arrangements.

After the service Tom decided to remain with me for a few days "to help you pick up the pieces," he said. He had taken leave from his job as a forestry professor at the University of British Columbia. My mother had not been able to come. She was hospitalized in Pennsylvania with a fractured hip. My sister and her husband planned to come from Vermont later to help me make plans for my family.

Tom became depressed and preoccupied; he spent hours talking with the attorneys and company officials. The president of Norm's company came to our house. He also constantly told twelve-year-old Normie: "You're the man of the house now." It was all so hellish—I wanted everyone to leave Tom and me alone with the children.

Tom decided to stay an extra week, and his gloom deepened. Whenever he looked at me his eyes filled with tears, and he would leave the room. We had both reached our nadir when he told me: "Mary dear, there's no company insurance." He went on to explain that there was a three-month grace period between Norm's job changes during which he was not insured. A strange use of the word, grace. The world is upside down, I thought.

"This is a dreadful thing to say," said Tom, tears rolling down his cheeks, "but if Norm had died six days later there would be over $80,000 company insurance.

As it is there's only his G.I. insurance of $10,000." The day before, mulling over how I could ever manage, I had said to myself, "Thank heavens for Norm's great business sense, and his bent for perfection." He planned carefully and felt secure, knowing that his company insurance protected his family.

Now another heavy black cloud hung over me. Tom and I sat up all night. It seemed that something should make it right. But there was no way. He had consulted with the company executives and attorneys and they said I was "out of luck." In addition, Tom had investigated Workmen's Compensation, but they would not recognize stress as one of the causative factors of heart attacks. Norm had jetted all over the country for the past three months negotiating end-of-the-year business for his company. But we were still in the dark ages of cardiac research. The menacing cloud would engulf me for some time.

Tom had to return to his work at the university. Apparently my sister and brothers had decided it would be helpful for me if John went with Tom to Vancouver. Suddenly our precious Johnnie was being whisked away from me for a visit with his aunt and uncle in Canada. I'll never know how it came about, how I consented to let him go; he had never been away from the bosom of our family. I was totally numb, I believe. "Only for a couple of months," my brother said, "just while you get some plans made." He said that their two children were looking forward to Johnnie's visit.

I was alone with four of my children, while my baby was flying away from me. At night sleep did not come. Lying in bed, empty and alone, on the raw edge of grief, I yearned for Norm. I did not want to stop thinking of him—I did not care if I could not sleep. The doctor had given me sedatives; I did not want them. The bottle was never opened; for years afterward it remained sealed and neglected in my medicine cabinet. Sometimes I looked at it and wondered why I had never discarded it.

Every day I went through the motions of caring for the children. I dragged myself to the supermarket in a daze; I missed Johnnie, his laughter, and felt incomplete. Yet I filled the basket, with the children's help. Normie, always sad, could not do enough. He made the lunch sandwiches in the morning, and made sure Peter and Mary got off on their bikes to school. He walked to the corner to catch his school bus. Dangling books in a strap, he walked tall and my heart went with him. At home with me, four-year-old George wanted to help me. He came to me as my head lay on my arms on the glass top of the white iron patio table. He took my head in his soft hands, and trying to smile, he pulled my face around to look into his eyes, saying, "I'm happy, Mommy." He would have done anything to make things the way they had been.

I was four years old when my father died, and my memory of the day after his funeral is indelible in my mind. Now I wrote letters to my mother trying to understand what had happened to me. Chains of inertia bound me in my chair. My neighbors and friends tried to comfort me. I could not leave my patio. I felt their helplessness.

One morning my next door neighbor brought me my mail from the roadside mailbox. She walked onto the patio where she knew I would be sitting. "I brought you some coffee, dear, and I'll take George across the street to play with the Simmons children if it's all right with you." I nodded and thanked her as she laid a large assortment of letters, mostly in white envelopes, in my lap. There was a letter from my mother. Her careful, neat, strong handwriting leaped out at me. Laying aside the other letters I tore open the one from Mother. Suddenly I gasped and crushed the letter into a firm ball and threw it across the patio. I cradled my head on my arms on the table, and felt my tears drenching my face and hands.

My crying gave way to sobbing, and then I seemed to regain a sense of reason. My mother really loves me, I thought. I stood up and walked to the edge of the patio to retrieve the crumpled ball that was my mother's letter. I gently and purposefully smoothed out the blue, wrinkled page. Almost caressing it, this time I thought about Mother's words as I read them. "One thing I cannot stand is self-pity," she wrote.

Mother was thirty-two years old when my father died and she had four young children, and what I remember the most about her was her irrepressible happiness. She had been born by the river, lived by the river, and when circumstances arose over which one had no control she loved to say, "Go with the river." She made the best of everything, even the bad times, the rough times. Now I knew that I would let go of my dam of self-pity; I had created a stagnant pool of despair, wallowing in it and going nowhere, and I was about to be mired in hopelessness. I went to the telephone and called Mother. We cried together, and we even laughed together that day I received her fateful letter.

That afternoon when the children came home from school I was in the front yard for the first time in weeks. Peter and Mary rode onto the driveway on their bikes. Mary, laying down her bike, watched me. She walked over and reached for my hand, looking up at me as she said, "Are you all right, Mom?" Peter rode across the grass straight to me. "Are you all right, Mom?" he asked, and hopped off his bike to hold my other hand. Seeing their worried eyes I smiled and said, "Yes, I'm all right." I saw a bit of relief in their faces, and they had a little bounce in their feet as they ran into the house with their books.

I remained awhile under the sheltering maple tree until I saw Normie walking up the street. When he saw me he drew back his shoulders and quickened his pace as he walked toward me. Oh, Normie, I thought, you don't have to walk so tall. He reached the maple tree, tossed his books on the ground, and asked me, "Are you all right, Mother?" I put my arm around him, and smiling I said, "Yes, Normie, I'm all right." I saw a hint of light come into his face that had been so darkened on that morning after Christmas. He picked up his books, and as we walked into the house together he said quietly, "You know, Mom, I think you really do seem better."

That evening I took the first bike ride I had taken since Norm died. I heard the hum of the wheels and the click of the odometer, I felt the rhythm of the ride, and I talked to myself. "What is the matter with you, Mary? My God, you certainly have a purpose, that *raison d'être* you say you always need. Get on with it, go with the river."

In my aloneness with my five children, I knew the task belonged to me. I had a constant conversation with myself: if I could just find a house large enough to house all my children, one not expensive, one that I could afford. If I could find a job with a salary to support my family. If I could use whatever strengths I possessed to find the best job possible—all possibilities—if I could do these things then I would be able to survive alone with my children. What strength I received from my mother; just a few words from a loving mother. I would find a house and a job. The following week I left my patio and made arrangements with friends in Palo Alto for a visit—to begin house hunting and job searching in Northern California. I decided not to go back to Pennsylvania but instead to return to the place where our family began and where our many friends were urging me to "come home again." Johnnie would return home as soon as I found a house.

Before Tom left he helped me estimate the Social Security and veterans' benefits available for my family. There would be no paycheck and I needed to determine how I would make ends meet. A letter came from Norm's company informing me that I would receive $750 a month for six months; they called it a kind of severance pay until I could get reestablished. Severance pay seemed an appropriate term. Tom and I figured that I could manage for several months, but by fall I would need to have a job that would pay me at least $6000 a year. That income along with the government benefits would provide the basic needs for my family. Immediately I had three tasks: to sell our home in Pittsburgh and find someplace to live in Palo Alto, to find a job, and to find someone to care for the children.

Early one morning, on awakening, I looked out at the dawn and for the first time I believe I was struck by the stark reality of being on my own again; it had finally registered somewhere deep within, probably in my soul. In that moment I knew that all I could do was take one day at a time, live in each moment, and go with the flow. And that evening, on one of my last bike rides in Palos Verdes, I thought of the river of my life with Norm and the children, and of my mother and her wisdom, her spirit, and her love. I was refreshed. Wasn't it the same river?

In April, after selling our home in Pittsburgh, I moved my family from Palos Verdes to Palo Alto. A good friend and neighbor, Harry Hall, worked with the realtor and managed to sell our house. By June I had found a job in school nursing and was enrolled in summer school at Stanford so I could qualify for a Health and Development teaching credential to ensure a permanent position. Fortunately I had my Certificate in Public Health Nursing from Simmons College and had gone to Stanford after I was discharged from the Army.

For the third task, someone to care for my children, a miracle did happen. Mrs. Anderson, a former baby sitter before we moved to Pittsburgh, agreed to help me during the summer, but she thought at the age of seventy-three she was too old to work full time when I started my job. During these years there were no child care centers, so I would need someone to come to my home to take care of John and George when school began in the fall. Mrs. Anderson offered to help interview applicants during the summer.

My eligibility for certain government programs was a life saver for me. Because I had served in the Army Nurse Corps, I could return to Stanford with financing from the G.I. Bill. In addition, I would receive Social Security and veterans' benefits for the children because of Norm's war injury. However, I had become a single woman—and had not been working—so I was unable to qualify for a mortgage, even with my Certificate of

Eligibility for a G.I. mortgage. Fortunately my sister and her husband underwrote my mortgage, and I was able to buy a small but adequate home in Palo Alto.

I would be troubled by many inequities in my life as a woman alone with children, not unlike those my mother faced in her job as a school nurse after my father died. Only unmarried women could be teachers or school nurses in the 1920s and 1930s. That rule had been changed when I became a school nurse, but there was another policy in regard to a woman alone. I could not qualify for the group life insurance which was available to other faculty members because I was a single woman—even though I was the head of the household of five children. As the water in a river eventually wears down a boulder over the years, so did the spirit and determination of single women with families finally change the rule and make their insurance coverage possible.

1962, Back Row: Norm, Jr., Mary, Sr.
Front Row: George, Mary, Jr., Peter, John

Alone with
Five Children

It was noontime when Joany, a golfing friend, and I approached the eighteenth tee at the Stanford Golf Course. Ours was a good foursome, and my game was showing improvement. This morning we had arrived early and were joined by two men who had low handicaps; we welcomed the challenge. We usually played weekly tournaments with our Stanford women's group, but this morning was a relaxed practice round.

I felt a new freedom in the fall of 1990. Retired and working only three days a week as a consultant for a drug abuse program in East Palo Alto, I discovered golf to be a meditative experience for me, a time when I could let go of all thoughts and focus on the little white ball. It seemed that golf was an appropriate metaphor for living life, for going with the flow. "Ping clubs give the best results," said John, my youngest son, when he gave them to me, "because they are the most forgiving." And so it is in life, I thought, the more forgiving people are of each other, the more enduring is their relationship. Another lesson about life was revealed when a golfing partner, preparing to drive her ball off the first tee, asked me to watch for her. "I can never see where they end," she said. As I lost her ball in the sunlight, I remarked, "Isn't that the way it is in this world? We usually can't see how things are going to end."

In the heart of an urban environment there is a kind of oasis and serenity on the fairways, a place to let go of the clutter in my life! On the Stanford Golf Course one is hardly aware of the highway lying below its first tee, or the nearby sprawling shopping center; although the fairways and greens have been manicured by man, the quintessence of nature prevails among the friendly foothills and great oaks and I feel a sense of peace.

From the top of the hill we could see the San Francisco skyline about thirty-five miles in the distance. Joany and I hit long drives on the final five-par hole and headed down the fairway, fatigued yet savoring the end of a morning's hike up and down the rugged terrain. My golf bag was heavy, slung over my shoulder and across my back; the clubs made rhythmic metal sounds as they knocked against each other on the downhill trek. Joany walked beside me, the clanking of her clubs keeping time with mine. "You know, Mary," she said, "I think you're the only woman I've ever played with who gives herself such praise after a good shot—oh, I don't mean to criticize you—it's just an observation."

I was embarrassed. "Do I really do that?" I asked, shifting my bag of clubs from one shoulder to the other. "How do I do that?" Joany laughed and said, "Whenever you have an unusually good shot you say, 'Way to go, Mary; that was great!' or 'Did you see that shot? Wow, I really nailed that one!' Sometimes when you sink a putt you exclaim, 'Fantastic, I really am a brilliant putter.' You see, Mary, it's just a conversation you seem to have with yourself. It's as though you constantly give yourself encouragement."

When Joany reached her ball she removed her bag from her shoulder, withdrew a club, and prepared to hit her third shot. She waggled her club in front of the ball, ready to hit, but stopped to look at me. She is a woman of average height, an attractive blond in khaki shorts, displaying legs that have the shape of youth and the crinkly skin of a grandmother who early in her life had tanned her body well. Suddenly she became serious, and her M.S. degree in Communications from Stanford took over. "Now don't get me wrong," she said. "I'm not finding fault. I do the same thing—all the time—just in the course of my everyday life. That's probably why I noticed you doing it here on the golf course." She lined up her club with the ball and her target, checked her grip, and after a slow back swing hit the ball straight and far, almost to the green. "See that!" she shouted. "Wasn't that great?"

"And how!" I said, watching her ball so clean and sweet. "You know, Joany, now that you've told me, and now that you've done it too, I understand; yes, I do pat myself on the back—a lot."

"That's right," Joany said, "and I'll tell you why. We've both been widows, alone with children, more than a few years. If we don't give ourselves a pat on the back once in awhile, who will?" She laughed and then asked me, "Whatever happened to the book you were writing, *Living Alone with Five Children*"? I replied that I continued to create it in my mind but rarely got it on paper. "It seems I've always been too busy," I said.

"Well," Joany said, "I knew what you meant by that title—thought it would probably be the story of my life also. You need to finish it."

As I drove home I thought about the book I started to write but never finished. I remembered my friends who tried to console me, after Norm had died, telling me how fortunate I was to have the children because I would not be alone. But I felt very alone, especially with a house full of children. I went to bed alone; it was the time I felt most alone. I talked about the children to myself or to their father who was not there, but often I sensed he listened to me, shared their ups and downs with me, in fact, helped me. But I missed the caresses, the tenderness of hands, the passion, the embraces that had become a habit, knowing that no matter how chaotic a day there would always be a kind of refuge before sleep. One can only *feel* the emptiness. There is no defining word; it centers somewhere inside, in the gut, in the chest, in the heart.

Major decisions became my bailiwick; there was no question about that. Even though family discussions with the children were plentiful, I was in charge. I had to earn the money and pay the bills, and I *was* the head of the household of four sons and one daughter. I was alone with children, and I began to write stories about that, but always there were interruptions.

❦

Sometimes I felt as though I was reenacting a scene from the past. I remembered as a small girl watching my mother—a widow with four young children—when she would seem to melt into the kitchen wall, her head resting on her arms while she cried, exploding with sobs for a few minutes, finally dropping her hands to grasp the edge of her apron and wipe her eyes. Then, looking at our worried faces, she would smile and say, "Oh, well, things have a way of working out." It was during the Depression and she could no longer charge our food at Milspaw's grocery down at the corner, a block from our home, because she couldn't pay the bill, but she did get credit at a store farther away. It seemed very far for my sister and me to walk, across the Fifth Street Bridge, down Water Street, along the creek to a store near the Third Street bridge. I remember that my face was hot, and it was hard for me to breathe when the storekeeper leaned over the counter and asked what we wanted; we had no money, just a request from our mother. But when my sister asked the storekeeper to charge the bread and potatoes, and he said, "Sure thing, I know your mother," I felt better.

❦

Those years when I was the sole support of my family, much of my frustration was related to money. I can still hear my children whispering to one another at the beginning of a month, on a Saturday morning, "Don't bother Mother; she's at the kitchen table doing the bills, and she's really in a bad mood." And probably, undoubtedly, I was feeling flushed and out of breath too. Not only did I sometimes cry against the wall, but one time, during a squabble between the two older boys I stood on a kitchen chair—to be taller than all the children—and announced, "I *am* the boss." But it resulted in laughter. "You look funny, Mom, standing up there," said one of my sons. And although I felt very much alone I laughed with them, and felt comforted by the laughter. Once I heard a quote, "Laughter is the highest form of prayer," and although I don't remember who said it, I had embraced that notion because it seemed to fit. When I laughed with the children or at myself, I was praying, praying that things weren't as tough as they seemed, or in my own mother's words, that things would have a way of working out.

When we lived in Pittsburgh, Pennsylvania, before moving to Palos Verdes where Norm died, our family had been members of the Mt. Lebanon Presbyterian Church, where we regularly attended Sunday School. Cliff Smith, the assistant minister, had been our Sunday School teacher and a good friend to Norm and me; he was one of the first people I called from California the morning Norm died. A few months later, after moving from Southern California to the Bay Area, I read in the *Palo Alto Times* that Dr. Cary Weisiger, the minister from the Mt. Lebanon church, was being transferred to the Menlo Park Presbyterian Church where my children had been baptized before our move to Pennsylvania.

Our association with the Mt. Lebanon church had already had a powerful effect on me. During the first week of my grief, when I was lost in despair, my oldest son, twelve-year-old Normie, placed my small leather-bound Bible on the kitchen table in front of me. He opened it to the page where the attached black ribbon lodged, and placed his finger on the fine print of a verse, Deuteronomy. Ch. 31, Vs. 6.

"Mom," he said, "Mr. Sefton, my Sunday School teacher, told us that if ever something happened that made us very sad, something really sad, and we didn't know what to do, to read this scripture." My eyes followed his finger as he read the words, *"Be strong and of good courage, fear not, nor be afraid of them: for the Lord, thy God, he it is that doth go with thee; he will not fail thee, nor forsake thee."* I would never forget that moment, or the verse, or that my son brought it to me.

A few months after Dr. Weisiger came to California, our friend, Cliff Smith, arrived to be his assistant minister. I felt it was an omen that our family was well cared for. I rejoined the Menlo Park Presbyterian Church and every Sunday, at eight o'clock in the morning, I sat in the front pew with my children before they were sent off to their various Sunday School classes. One morning Dr. Weisiger stood behind the pulpit, lifted up his great Bible, and said to the children, "This is God's book," and then he placed it squarely in front of him while he read a scripture. As we left the church that morning we passed Dr. Weisiger, and four-year-old George said, "There goes God."

After several months of this schedule I had an ambivalence about going to church. Cliff Smith visited us at Christmastime, brought us a five-pound box of See's candy. He remarked about how handsome my children were, how well behaved they were. In the warmth of my home, I confided in him, "You should see my house on Sunday mornings when I'm getting everyone ready for Sunday School," I told him. "I'm at my wits' end—shirts that don't fit or are unironed, ties that don't tie, socks that don't match, and just the right dress for my daughter—and behavior that I can't describe. Frankly, I'm so tired of it all." Reverend Smith seemed to hear me, so I continued talking, almost crying. "In a nutshell, Cliff, I act very un-Christian on Sunday mornings." I was relieved when he suggested that perhaps I should let up on Sunday School for awhile, that perhaps I had just too much to do. And so I took his advice. I continued to read the Bible, and I prayed a lot, and I hung onto the belief that indeed the greatest strength that I possessed was the spirit within, and I cherished and thanked God for the laughter in my home. The current in the stream of my life was sometimes so swift and changing, that all I was able to do was just go with the river.

A miracle did occur when I searched for someone to care for the children while I looked for a job and attended Stanford to earn a teaching credential. Shortly after our arrival in Palo Alto I drove over to visit Mrs. Anderson, who had been our occasional baby sitter in Menlo Park before we moved to Pennsylvania. In those days all the mothers on our street had coveted Mrs. Anderson, "a good woman who took good care of kids." Usually our young families watched over each other's children, but for special occasions we vied with each other for her services.

Mrs. Anderson lived in a trailer park on Frontage Road, parallel with the Bayshore Freeway. When I parked our station wagon, loaded with my family, in front of her immaculate trailer she was sitting on her grassy spot in a deck chair knitting. "Land sakes," she cried out, as she stood up and walked toward our car, "where did you all come from?" When I told her about Norm's death and my need for help, she hugged me hard and long, and carefully surveyed each child as he or she tumbled out of the familiar blue Ford station wagon. "They've grown so tall," she said, wiping away tears, as she led Johnnie and George into her trailer to bring out cookies. It seemed as though we had come home. "So hard to believe," she said as she lifted up Johnnie. "Look at him; he was only six weeks and six pounds when you left California!"

I told her that I was going to summer school at Stanford to qualify for a Health and Development credential. "I need someone to take care of the children this summer and when I start work in the fall."

"Well," she hesitated and folded her hands in her lap, "you know I'm seventy-three years old, and I'm retired from caring for children. Decided I'm too old, so I'm just taking care of my trailer and my flowers. Sometimes it feels like I'm still out there on the strip in Arizona. Just like that was, this's home to me and I'll just putter out my life here, listening to the birds in my yard and the cars on the freeway." The Arizona Strip was a part of that state where she had lived with her husband, Mr. Anderson, before he died many years ago. He used to "run cattle," she said. They had no children, and she helped him with the roadside tourist operation which provided their livelihood. My children remembered the hair-raising cowboy stories she used to tell when she was the baby sitter in our old neighborhood.

I explained to Mrs. Anderson that I had already signed up for classes at Stanford, and I would need her only a few hours a day during the summer. "It would be so wonderful if you'd just come during the summer," I said, and sensed her weakening. "Please ride home with us for a minute. I want to show you where we live now—it's easy to get there from here." She agreed that she did want to see our house, and "Lord knows it's a treat to be with you all." In a few minutes we drove up to our house, tucked away at the end of a cul-de-sac. Practical and decisive as always, Mrs. Laura Anderson suddenly announced to me as she slid out of the front seat and stood facing me, "I'll do it for you, just for these summer months while you get that schooling. You just tell me the days, the hours you need me, Mary, and I'll be here." It all happened so easily, miraculously, and later when school started I placed an ad to find someone to take over for Mrs. Anderson in September.

Mrs. Anderson offered to screen the applicants in order to save me time. She would talk to them on the telephone and if they sounded like "someone reliable, someone with some sense" she would invite them over so she could "check them out personally" before I interviewed them. "A woman came today," she said, "and I just didn't have good vibes, and also she had dirty fingernails." And the next day when another person answered the ad, she reported, "She was too young, and she had a little two-year-old girl that she had to bring with her. I'd liked to have helped her, but you don't need an extra child here." And so it continued with her turning away applicants until she said, "No one can take care of 'my children.' I need to do it myself! I'll just stay on when you go to work." So another problem was settled; I no longer had to worry about who would care for my children when I started my job.

I needed to be in my health office in the high school every morning at 8 A.M. Mrs. Anderson would arrive at my house weekday mornings at 7:15 A.M., slowly driving her gray Studebaker Lark toward the wide end of the cul-de-sac to park under the tree in front of our house. She was of medium height with narrow shoulders and broad hips. Her long gray hair was tightly braided and circled her head like a crown, held firmly in place with pearl-colored combs which she frequently adjusted to tuck in an unruly hair. She always wore print dresses with full, long skirts and sturdy black-laced shoes. She carried a heavy brocaded purse, loaded with her "essentials": a screwdriver, tweezers, scissors, ribbons, band aids, clippers to trim the roses in the backyard, and a variety of treats. She was always on time, and she never missed a day.

The children came home from school at lunch time for hot potato cakes or her special stew. They went to school with patches on their jeans, not ironed on but carefully sewn with strong stitches. We had acquired a kind, storybook grandmother, and I knew I was blessed to have her with me during those first years that I was alone with my children. But it would not last.

One day in early June, the year that John would begin kindergarten in September, Mrs. Anderson asked me to come and visit her in her trailer in the evening. "Come by yourself so we can talk," she said. When I arrived she asked me to sit down at her tiny table, covered with a daisy print tablecloth. We sat in the built-in seats of her trailer kitchen with our knees almost touching while she poured two cups of steaming Sanka. I was sipping the decaf when she said, "I don't think you'll need me anymore." I swallowed hard and felt the hot liquid in my throat and chest. She continued, "Johnnie and George will both be in school next year, and with Mary in fifth grade, Peter in junior high, and Normie in high school seems like you're all set now. One of the older ones can be there until you get home from work."

She wriggled out from behind her table and pulled open a drawer in the narrow chest that was part of the wall. "And I'm planning to get married." She removed a tiny blue box from the drawer and handed it to me. Her expression didn't change much but I distinctly felt a change in her. Inside the box was a shiny gold band nestled in the crevice of the white velvet lining. As Mrs. Anderson lifted it out and held it closer for me to see it better, I sensed in her soft breathing a hint of laughter, the expectancy of a young bride. It all seemed to happen in that split second, and I was struck numb by the fact that our seventy-six-year-old "grandmother" was moving on.

"Henry had it to show me when he proposed to me yesterday, Sunday." She was holding the ring in the palm of her hand. My first reaction was one of wonderment and disbelief. She had never told me that her friend, Henry Buck, who lived in an adjacent trailer in the Woodland Trailer Park, was any more than a friend. He was a pleasant eighty-year-old gentleman who had invented a golf putter which he called, "Buck's bucker." He was trying to market it but was having trouble because as he said, "It's not conventional, you know, and they say it's illegal because you have to hit it by facing the hole, swing it between your legs, like a croquet mallet." Mrs. Anderson would say, "It's nonsense, don't listen to him; it'll never sell."

Now she confided in me that he was really "a wonderful man, kind, and very intelligent," and although she never thought she'd marry again this seemed right for her. "Mary, I want you to know that Henry has *never* been in my trailer without a third person being here. Usually Mrs. Miller or another neighbor comes to have dinner with us, but I've never been in my trailer alone with Mr. Buck. He's a very respectful man, and, of course, I wouldn't allow it!"

Laura Anderson and Henry Buck were married in a private ceremony, and my family and neighbors toasted them with champagne at a party in our cul-de-sac before they motored to Vermont, his home state, for their honeymoon. Three weeks later they drove through Oregon on their way back to California. When they arrived home in their trailer camp Mrs. Anderson called me to tell me that they had had a wonderful time. "And guess what happened on our honeymoon?" she asked. When I responded, "Don't tell me you're pregnant!" she chuckled and said, "Heavens no! But we did buy a ranch just outside Medford."

Mrs. Anderson was proud that she had earned a pension. The Social Security payments I made during those years she cared for my children made her eligible for retirement benefits; at her age she needed to work only eight quarters in order to qualify. (Years later, when Mrs. Anderson died at age ninety-four, I would discover her birthdate on the notice of her memorial service, and realize that she had been seventy-six years old when she came to work for our family, and nearly eighty when she married Mr. Buck. Her niece said that she thought both her aunt and Henry lied about their ages so that the other would be more interested in marriage.) When Mrs. Anderson received her first Social Security check she invited our family out for dinner to celebrate. There was much to honor; I would always revere the healing presence of Mrs. Anderson during those tender years. It strengthened me for what was yet to come.

As the children grew older, and my job more stressful, life became more complicated. Although I believed in going with the flow, there were moments when I seemed to lose all reason, and just wanted to abandon the river. Often my patience was exhausted when our family sat down for the evening meal. I would sit at the head of the table with my oldest son Norm, fifteen, at the other end with Peter and Mary on one side and George and John on the other. Sometimes I would lose my poise completely with the interchange of teasing or just plain silliness and would demand that everyone be silent and simply "eat your dinner, no talk, just eat!" One of these times, John, now in first grade, looked around the table, felt the silence and my unhappiness, and said, "Anyone at this table who likes Mother, raise your hand." He had his hand halfway raised, but when no one raised a hand, he lowered his. He was outnumbered.

After dinner seven-year-old George came into the kitchen and heard me talking to myself. His eyes opened wide when he saw no one else in the kitchen and his face reddened as he came over to the sink where I was washing dishes. "Did you say something, Mom?" he asked, "or did someone just leave?" "No, George," I said. "Oh, no, I was just talking to myself—I'm the only one in this family who understands me."

I had an old wing chair in my bedroom which became my place of meditation, prayer, deep thinking, inner dialogue, and just plain talking to myself. A woman alone talks to herself a lot. My chair, upholstered in linen, an old-English flowered pattern of muted colors, was my refuge, my quiet place where I believed I touched my soul.

And then there were those times when I was desperate to get away completely from the children and the house, from the total confusion, frustration, and pressure. I needed to escape, to get away from petty problems: a lost baseball mitt, the displeasure of my daughter about my "lack of interest" in the height of the heels on her new shoes, or accusations of not listening to "both sides" of an argument between siblings. But most of all, I believe, it was the activity, the din, the noise—the energy of having five growing children in a house at the end of a day when I was already emotionally spent—that propelled me out of the house. I would walk into the garage and grab my bicycle, my three-speed Schwinn which I had ridden around the tenements of Boston when I was a twenty-year-old public health nurse. "I'm going for a bike ride," I would announce to whomever was in earshot. I would wheel down the driveway, not looking back, driven by a force within me that was firmly saying, "just go." On these rides there welled up within me great surges of bursting freedom, freedom to be by myself, to be alone. The surges were so powerful that I needed to go. Even in the rain I needed to leave on my bike.

Other times I escaped in my car, to be alone, to think. I would find myself driving around the block, almost blindly, with soulful sobbing and torrents of tears, asking myself how I could survive all the complications and demands of raising my family. But the car did not help; I felt more trapped.

What a tonic my bicycle turned out to be: just the need to pedal, to use my energy to go forward into nowhere in particular. I felt the wind and the breeze or the rain against my face, in my hair—it was as though I was being caressed. The speed of the ride balanced my faithful Schwinn and for a moment my hands left the handlebars, free and light as I held them aloft, unencumbered, the soft air of the night rippling through my fingers. The cluttered thoughts, stagnated in weariness, seemed to float away. As my bike lost speed I bent forward to grip the handlebars again and pedaled vigorously up a road that curved around the creek.

In those days in Palo Alto few people rode bicycles. High school students considered it "uncool"; they all walked no matter what the distance, unless of course a friend had a car. I had a small chrome light on the handlebars because my oldest son thought I should not ride in the dark without a light. Sometimes I didn't want to flick it on when darkness came; I wanted to be invisible.

I felt a serenity, but also an emptiness, in the deep darkness along the creek, like being on the edge of the woods, not knowing what was beyond. Straggly trees hovered above sprawling shrubs on the briar-covered bank that plunged downward toward the creekbed, dark and damp and forbidding.

The houses I passed sat quietly with lights glowing in kitchens and front rooms. They appeared peaceful; there was an occasional flicker of a television. It seemed as though the mood within those houses was tranquil, that two parents were quietly interacting with their children. But that thought only crossed my mind; I knew better. I listened to tales of home life daily in the private confines of my nurse's office: a sixteen-year-old girl afraid to tell her mother that she had missed a period, a football player who carried his drunken father from the front sidewalk into his house once or twice a week, a mother who had left her family and they didn't know where she was, worried parents who had found drugs in dresser drawers, a boy who wouldn't leave his bedroom all day. Day after day: a girl who continuously dug into the flesh on the inner part of her arms, a freshman boy afraid of P. E. and his father.

Farther away, on the other side of the narrow creek, a few houses also beckoned with lights, dimly twinkling through trees, remote, and I needed to go home to my house full of children on 50 Jordan Place. It was during these bicycle rides that I could tap an inner peace and let go of the anger and the blame that I had begun to heap upon my children. Even the dissonance that prevailed among the faculty and administration in our school district seemed to float away. The only voice I heard was my own, asking myself questions, beseeching whatever power there be for wisdom. In the silence I found an energy, a resilience, as though I had been recharged. When I was able to savor my aloneness, life became easier; it seemed that I could throw myself, almost with abandon, into living with my children, loving them, enjoying them, and at the same time, dealing with the dilemmas that were part of my job.

And I learned from children, both in school and at home. One of the students brought a stray puppy to school and in turn I brought her home for my youngest son John. He had longed for a dog, and his care and discipline of Tasha proved to be a lesson in love and responsibility. John also had a paper route which he attended to and managed with uncommon ease; in the darkness of every morning I would hear him slide open the door to the garage where he folded his papers before delivery. Almost an hour later—after completing his route on his bicycle, accompanied by Tasha—I would hear him tip-toeing down the hall to return to his bed. When he came out to breakfast one morning I said to him, "How do you manage that, John, never failing to get up early to deliver your papers, yet able to return to sleep again." He laughed and said, "I hardly know the guy that gets up with the alarm and delivers the papers in the dark, he just does it. I'm the one who gets up in the daylight to go to school."

During the sixties the problems that arose in my health office became more complex as the "flower children"—wild flowers in the garden of our youth—took root and sprouted, spreading with tendrils of freedom and rebellion. They renounced the Vietnam War and rebelled against parents and adults. This challenge of our youth was great; parents and adults scurried about to create ways to bring children back into the fold. The scheduling of classes in high schools lost structure and became so flexible that students could create their own programs daily; some created programs with no classes. Much of my time was spent with parents, tracking down their children, trying to determine if they were using drugs. Marijuana was the favorite drug for abuse, but students were also passing out on campus with the overdoses of "reds" (Seconal) and "whites" (amphetamines). School personnel needed to be educated about these drugs; the police department shared their expertise in faculty workshops, displaying living marijuana plants as well as the dried, ready-to-smoke leaves.

An advantage of my household full of children was that I could quickly relate to other parents, often facing the same frustrations they experienced. I recall praising one of my sons because he watered and nurtured the flowers around my back patio, even got up early in the morning to attend to the task. In fact, I bragged a bit when I told a neighbor how diligently he worked in my garden. One morning after breakfast I stepped outside, enjoying my final cup of coffee as I walked beside the flower beds. Suddenly I noticed among the awakening California poppies and the brilliant marigolds an unfamiliar plant—its leaves had five points. On close inspection I realized the plant was similar to the specimen the police officer had brought to our drug abuse workshop. When I went back into the house I found that everyone had left for school. Trembling with disbelief, I drove to my office. I was too distraught and ashamed to mention it to anyone and waited until noon to go home and be there when my son came for lunch.

As soon as he entered the kitchen my verbal attack began. "Do you realize that your mother could be charged with a felony for growing marijuana in her backyard?" I was furious and we both headed for the patio, determined to eradicate the problem at once. I raged through the flower bed, pulling up plants and tossing them on a newspaper. With his chin on his chest, shoulders drooping, my son followed me, reluctantly removing the lush plants from the moist earth, laying them carefully on the heap I had jerked from the bed of marigolds. Finally they were securely enshrouded in newspaper and disposed of in the garbage can. "And that is that!" I declared, and my son said, "I know, Mom."

My fury had not abated when I came home from school at the end of the day, and a little voice inside sent me to check the garbage can. The newspaper package of plants had disappeared. Again I waited for my son to come home. My heart was pounding. Overwhelmed with disappointment, I sat at the kitchen table looking out the window. Finally, after baseball practice, he arrived. I ushered him into the side yard, and before I had lifted the lid of the garbage can, he rubbed his eyes and said, "I'm sorry, Mom, I'm really sorry, but, Mom, it took so long to grow those plants; I just wanted to see if they were any good." That was one of the times I felt totally inadequate. It was one of the times I simply went to bed and cried, and the shedding of tears seemed to help.

Perhaps my experiences facilitated communication with the parents I counseled, but my daily family dilemmas were my own to solve. I had to make the necessary decisions, and I was never sure I made the right ones, and still I don't know, but I'm still with the river.

Childhood illnesses consume a working mother. When the children are well and head off for school with filled lunch boxes in the morning the working day goes well. But earaches, chest colds, or communicable diseases that come and go, all these require children to remain at home while mother works. Sometimes the older one must stay home to care for a younger child, and luckily I had a neighbor who would look in on them. Mainly it is time going by that helps because children become old enough to be left alone, home in bed. But I reached my lowest depression when George became ill at the age of fourteen.

George was the pride of our family on the junior tennis circuit; he had been a top-ranked player in his age group since the age of nine, a protégé of Nick Carter—the Pied Piper of tennis at the Foothills Tennis Club. He won the Washington State Championship and the National Canadian Open in both singles and doubles when he was fourteen years old. Shortly after those successes he came home from a tennis tournament one day and stood in the kitchen, tall, suntanned, and downcast, pointing to his swollen knees. "Look, Mom, look what's happened to my knees; they really hurt," he said. I tried not to act alarmed when I saw the swelling in his long, muscular legs but I knew something was very wrong and called our family doctor for an immediate appointment. Many blood tests and x-rays followed but the diagnosis remained uncertain. We never knew whether it was juvenile rheumatoid arthritis or his body's response to rapid growth—six feet tall at fourteen— along with the intense physical exercise on concrete tennis courts. Something had raised havoc with his immune system.

Weeks of internal panic stretched into months as I prayed for George's health, our family almost drowning in a flood of despair. The treatment was complete bed rest along with extremely high doses of aspirin. A home teacher came every day, as George began his high school studies in bed. I thought those dark days would never pass when I drove off to school every morning leaving George home alone, bedridden. And always on my return at noon and after school I tried to will him well. "Are you feeling better, George? I think the swelling is less." At night on my bike rides I rode along the creek with tears streaming down my cheeks, praying for strength to deal with my despair.

Finally his illness seemed to be in remission, and George was able to go to school on crutches. He was reluctant to return in such a state, and I'll always remember the encouragement of my dear friend, Jean Jones, who transported him to and from school until the swelling subsided and he was able to walk on his own again. The gloom and depression that engulfed our family that year evaporated, and George's good humor prevailed. He later said he became a better student while on home teaching. And more recently when I quoted my mother's oft-said advice, "go with the river," George reminded me of a similar metaphor in a novel he had read while in high school, Hermann Hesse's *Siddhartha*.

The river is everywhere at the same time, at the source, and at the mouth, at the waterfall, at the current, in the ocean and in the mountains, everywhere, and that the present only exists for it, not the shadow of the past nor the shadow of the future.

> *"That is it,"* said Siddhartha, *"and when I learned that, I reviewed my life and it was also a river, the boy, the mature man, the old man, were only separated by shadows, not through reality."*

Finally I look at *my* river, the little girl who watched her mother, the full woman in the flow of life with her children, and the grandmother who writes her stories, the same veiled spirit.

Our family in 1971

*George at Foothills
Tennis Club, 1969*

Ginny, Tom,
John David,
and Mary
with Mother,
1924

Cully

Aunt Johnetta

A Portrait of
My Mother

Pack up all my cares and woe, here I go,
Singing low, Bye Bye Blackbird.
No one here can love and understand me,
Oh what hard luck stories they all hand me,
—Blackbird, Bye Bye—

In the spring of 1969 my mother lived alone in Warren, Pennsylvania, and I was busy with my five children and my job as school nurse in a high school district in California. But the distance between us was of little consequence. Mother always seemed to call me just when I needed to hear from her. One time she called when I was stymied with a problem in statistics at Stanford. (I took courses in the graduate school of education during my summer vacations in order to advance on the salary schedule.) "I've been thinking about your statistics problems, Mary. You know, the theory of probability has always intrigued me."

As she spoke I scribbled and erased on my note pad, not listening very intently. It was difficult for me to believe that Mother was offering to help me with a statistics problem, but she knew it had troubled me.

"It's like a game," she said. "That's why I enjoy my bridge so much. Don't you see? Think of it as a game, my dear, and you'll be able to relax and get your problem solved. It's fun."

Somehow I passed that course. Her incredible lightness had spurred me on. Needless to say, I was not prepared for the diagnosis of *precocious senility* that the doctors in the nursing home would write on her chart during the next few months.

Mother was seventy-nine and had serious health problems. Mainly, her heart was failing, yet her conversations with me were spirited and continuously bolstered my morale. She had moved from her home, a small farm bordering the Allegheny River, into town a few years ago after Cully, my stepfather, died. Her apartment was clearly her own invention. Always she had been able to devise an environment of comfort, color, cheerfulness, and charm. She had done it again in the Warren Apartments, next door to the public library. With the enthusiasm of a new bride, she created a lovely place to spend her declining years, as she called them. A comfortable old carpet-back rocker settled on a domestic oriental rug, along with some appealing modern furniture gracing her small living room. The family pictures and her collection of books in the built-in bookcases rendered a restful nostalgia. She loved being next door to the library. A basket of books sat on the table near the front door—they were either coming or going.

I knew that Mother missed the farm in Pleasant Township where she had lived for many years with Cully, my stepfather, and where she had a reputation for being one of the best flower growers for miles around. She knew her flowers well, not only by their popular names but she often spoke to them, addressing them in Latin. Once she ordered from the Wayside Nursery a dozen special hybrid roses; she talked to them daily and cared for them well, but they gradually withered and died, one by one. She wrote to the nursery explaining her care of them, how she had talked to them regularly, and yet they died. She received not only a dozen new rose bushes but also a special plant which the nursery said "thrives on conversation."

But Mother was forever resourceful and had many interests. She seemed to have adjusted to life in town very well. As she had been one of the original duplicate bridge players in Warren, it was easy for her to continue her habit of playing every Monday night. Her partners were young and old and she was consistently in demand for a game. Active in the theater guild and possessing perfect pitch, she had starred in musicals and had played

Sophie Tucker in a one-person show when she was seventy years old.

"Never expect anything in return from those you may be able to help," Mother would say. "Your reward will come from some other person in some form you'll never expect. Just give what you want and when and to whom you want—do it cheerfully and forget about it."

She was able to be a friend in many unusual ways, and most people never knew about her good deeds. A young married woman who helped her with household chores had eight children. She mentioned to Mother that her husband had read an article about vasectomies and thought it would be a good method of birth control for their burgeoning family but it was very expensive. "Let me pay for Homer's vasectomy," Mother said. And she did.

Mother had an old hip fracture which she had refused to allow the doctors to repair. (She usually rejected doctors and their advice.) So she had to walk with a crutch. She purchased a sporty Pontiac Firebird to improve her mobility. Mother didn't like to hear people complain, or to focus on health problems.

"Why do you limp so, Anne?" a friend asked.

"Because I like to!" she snapped back to end that conversation.

Or her friend, Elsie, bemoaning all the illnesses of their mutual friends, said, "Oh, Anne, did you hear about

Hulda's terrible arthritis? And isn't it sad about poor Ivadel, poor thing? It's her back again."

And then Mother's abrupt response, "Elsie, do you know anyone who is *well?*"

Because Mother was a seemingly ageless woman, I didn't worry very much or too long about her even when she was experiencing some symptoms of heart congestion. Therefore it was a great shock to me when my brother, John David, called to tell me that Mother had been admitted to the hospital in a state of disorientation. After several weeks the doctors diagnosed her as having precocious senility. I wanted to fly back east and take care of my mother; I remembered how she recovered from pneumonia when I was single, a public health nurse in Boston; I took time off from my job—was able to drop everything to go home and nurse her back to health. But this time one of my children was bedridden with an extended illness, and also the demands of my job were so great that I really could not go. In frustrating talks on the telephone I questioned my brother and the doctor about her diagnosis, but they minimized my concern. I said to John, "I've never heard of such a thing. Where do they get that combination of words, precocious and senility? Mother's already old enough to become senile, so if that were the case, it wouldn't be precocious! And also senility doesn't usually happen overnight!"

"I know, I know," John tried to reassure me, "but these doctors know what they're talking about; they know what they're doing. She's almost uncontrollable. They've put her on medication to calm her down."

A few weeks later John called to say that Mother had been admitted to a nursing home. "They say that with this diagnosis of precocious senility there's no hope for recovery, and this seems like the best place for her. The doctors say it's not necessary for you to come now, Mary. They're doing all that can be done. I'll make the arrangements. Don't you worry."

As months went by I realized that everyone just assumed that Mother was going to be "out of it" for the rest of her life. I felt cheated because I could not fly back to Warren and take care of her. Part of me could not accept what was happening to my mother, and that part of me kept expecting her to call. Although I was told that her condition was permanent, I held on to the idea that it was temporary. At night when my house was quiet I would talk to my mother and I could hear her answers as though she were there, and it comforted me. In the reality of daytime I plunged back into the turbulence of my teen-aged family and job, but thoughts of my mother and visions of her life were constantly with me. I continued to reject the fact that she had suddenly become senile. Only a week or so before she was hospitalized we had been talking about statistics—how could the condition develop so rapidly?

❦

My mother, Anna Gander, was born in the section of Warren, Pennsylvania called Gladerun; the Gladerun Creek flowed into the Allegheny River in the eastern part of town. My mother grew up and went to school there until she was twelve years old, when she had to quit school in the eighth grade to keep house for her father. Her most prized possession was her report card from elementary school. "I treasure this little grade book," she had said fairly recently, taking it from the top drawer of her bureau, "because it has the signatures of both my mother and father—and how I loved going to school!" The tan, tattered grade book is something to behold: *Scholars Monthly Reports* of Anna Gander, a PUPIL of Seventh Grade, Gladerun School, August 29, 1904. It reveals perfect attendance, grades in the 95th percentile with an abundance of 100s. She also received marks of 100 percent in "application" and "behavior"; the record ends with the Certificate of Promotion to the eighth grade in April 1905. How heartbroken she must have been not to be able to continue her schooling. But she dearly loved her father, and she took care of him until he died when she was sixteen years old.

After his death she had no home, so she went into the local training school for nurses. In those days a young girl could get into nurses' training in the Warren General Hospital without a high school diploma. The hospital nurses' quarters became her home. I have a three-page poem she wrote about the nurses in her class; way ahead of time she had foreseen bottled water in this verse:

> *Then we say to Hulda, what is your "water-brand"?*
> *She'll proudly say—the Glade-run creek,*
> *Where purest water's canned.*

Mother married my father when she graduated from nurses' training. She was nineteen, and he was twenty-seven. My father, Tom Wright, had been working for Bell Telephone since he was fourteen years old. "The smartest and most handsome man in town," Mother said. My sister and I knew by heart the pictures in the thick photograph album of their courtship and marriage. Smiling broadly on their honeymoon, they stood on the steps of the Lincoln Memorial, my father, tall and impressive with a homburg in hand, and Mother in a stylish suit, waist tiny, and a large-brimmed hat. How she loved hats! "Gives a person a lift," she would say, and during the Depression when times were the toughest she would flaunt a new hat. "We may be broke, but we aren't poor!"

My mother and father had moved into a two-story clapboard house, shaded by a great oak tree, on Brook Street in Warren, shortly after their marriage. Our family grew: two sons and two daughters, each almost two years apart in age. The Northern Spy apple trees which my father had planted in our backyard when my oldest brother, Tom, was born yielded their first crop of apples when Tom was eight years old. It was the year my father died.

My father had become ill following the flu epidemic in the 1920s, and developed diabetes. He wasted away from the disease because there was no treatment; insulin was discovered the year of his death, 1923. Mother was thirty-two years old then.

Mother knew she must get a job in order to take care of her four children. She wrote to Isabelle Stewart, who was a national leader in nursing and the Superintendent of Columbia University Nurses' Training School in New York. "Is it possible that a university would accept me in a public health nursing program without a high school diploma?" she inquired. Miss Stewart referred her to Washington University in St. Louis, Missouri. I remember Mother singing and dancing around the kitchen when the letter came, and she said she was going to St. Louis. "Pack up all my cares and woe, here I go, singing low, Bye Bye Blackbird."

Proceeds from a small Bell Telephone Company insurance policy were adequate to pay for her university course. Aunt Johnetta, my father's youngest sister, came from Virginia to take care of us for a year while Mother was at the university. We were fortunate to have a loving aunt with us during that year while Mother earned her

Certificate in Public Health Nursing. She was given the job as school nurse in our home town immediately upon her return from St. Louis.

Later in life Mother married again; she married Carl Hultberg, her beau of long standing. Because she was the school nurse in our town, she could not marry because only single women were allowed to be teachers or nurses in schools. She would have lost her job if she had married. So Carl, or Cully, as we called him, was Mother's beau for quite a number of years while we were growing up. Finally in 1941 Mother and Cully were married.

Cully always had difficulty finding jobs because of the Depression, and he sometimes drank too much alcohol. (I have always abhorred small flat bottles, so easily concealed in so many places.) My sister, Ginny, and I knew though that Mother and Cully were in love. Discreet as they tried to be, we were aware of their love-making on the davenport in the living room.

Cully was in the infantry during World War I and met my mother when he returned from action in France. He was a handsome and cheerful man whom Ginny and I really counted on, as did our two brothers. He gave us haircuts when we needed them, and resoled our shoes when they had holes. He taught the boys about the woods and to hunt and fish. Cully could draw well, and I recall how he drew striking barbed wire fences along the pages of my English poetry project, "Barbs of Satire." He was an unusually bright and kind man.

The youngest son of a prominent family in town, Cully inherited some stock in the Corry-Jamestown Furniture Company. "That's our nest egg, Annie," he said to Mother. He could never sell the stock because it was tied up legally by other family members for many years. But he knew that money simply ran through Mother's fingers, as well as his own, and he was probably relieved that it was inaccessible. I believe he counted on it being there to take care of Mother in her declining years, and it was.

Because of a severe circulatory disease in the last years of his life, Cully had to have one of his legs amputated. Mother was devoted to him. "No Veterans Hospital for Carl," she would say, "not as long as I can take care of him." And she cared for him until he died.

The Corry-Jamestown stock had been depressed, and it was not until after his death that Mother realized the value of his "nest egg." Several months after Cully died, two men in business suits came down to the farm to ask Mother if she would sell her stock. "We can pay you the money right away," they promised her. She was about to accept their offer but my brother-in-law's better judgment caused her to wait. It turned out then, a few weeks later, that Corry-Jamestown stock was being bought by Singer Corporation and in a matter of months the value of the stock increased greatly. This enabled Mother to have a little bonanza and some security for the first time in her life; always before, she had lived on little money, just getting by. It was as though her habit of spooning off the bubbles in her coffee for good luck all the years of her life had finally paid off. In recent years, she delighted in entertaining her friends, telling them it was "compliments of Mr. Singer."

❦

Months went by, and I continued to question Mother's diagnosis, but only in my mind. My cousin, Marguerite, who visited her often, wrote to me that every once in awhile she would see a glimmer of my mother the way she used to be. Marguerite was a cousin and also one of Mother's best friends. Apparently when the medication started to wear off, Mother's sense of humor would come through: "She gets that old twinkle back in her eyes, Mary," Marguerite told me, "and today she said she wished her doctor was as good a doctor as he was a bridge player." It was becoming more and more difficult for Marguerite to believe that my mother had this senility they ascribed to her.

My Aunt Johnetta was on the evening nursing staff at the nursing home. She possessed a strong religious faith and a habit of humming and singing hymns as she worked among her dazed and lethargic patients: "I come to the garden alone, and the dew is still on the roses." "…He walks with me, and He talks with me and He tells me I am His own…" or "He leadeth me, He leadeth me, by His own hand He leadeth me." Aunt Johnetta knew Mother well and sensed that her intelligence and quick wit were battling to be liberated. Canvas straps buckled my mother to her bed all day. One evening Aunt Johnetta removed them to place Mother in a chair while she made her bed. Afterward she looked throughout the room for the straps until Mother laughed and pointed to the wastebasket where she had discarded them.

Aunt Johnetta, being a "take charge" kind of person, decided to omit Mother's medication during her duty time on the night shift. Without so much medication my mother's behavior began to change. Later Mother would tell me about these times. "I looked over at the bed beside me and said to myself, Isn't that Maud Higgins who has been in that 'home' for years? And isn't that poor old Nell Hodge who stopped talking so long ago?" Vaguely it came through to Mother that she also had been "put away."

"It was Johnetta singing hymns that made me start thinking. I tried to say the Lord's Prayer and couldn't remember the words. I became obsessed with the desire to remember every line."

Mother said it took her many difficult days to bring back each line, but finally she recalled it all. She started talking to Aunt Johnetta, and remembering. Fragile, yet resolute, she emerged from the darkness of her "senility" to make that record clear. She was then able to tell the doctors that she had fallen from her bed at home as she reached for the telephone on her bedside table. Apparently she had suffered a concussion which they had not recognized. They had simply treated her disorientation with medication. Mother was allergic to many drugs, yet when she objected vigorously to swallowing pills, they called it "acting-out" behavior, according to her medical records. The doctors then transferred her to the nursing home, where they continued a routine of various drugs causing her to be a zombie most of the time.

Several months had passed when Cousin Marguerite wrote to me in California, "I think it's important that you come to see your mother. She's asking for you." My brother John David could hardly believe her improvement; the doctors had said her condition was permanent and gave no hope. But when Mother said, "Get some of my money out of the bank and buy Mary a ticket so she can come to see me," he was elated. He knew she was back in action. I applied for an emergency leave from my job, and a friend took care of my family for me.

When Mother learned I was on my way to her, she began helping in the nursing home, combing patients' hair and talking with those who were lonely and remote. Aunt Johnetta had convinced the doctors to discontinue her medication; fortunately Aunt Johnetta was an impressive woman, and the doctors listened to her. What a stand she took for my mother, and how attentive and perceptive was Cousin Marguerite. I felt a sadness for all those patients who do not have an Aunt Johnetta or a Cousin Marguerite in their lives.

I received a letter from Mother. "I'm planning for you to get me out when you come." It was like I was part of a conspiracy, and how I looked forward to that when I boarded a plane in San Francisco!

I arrived in Warren in February of 1970. Warren is in the "snow belt": frigid air blows off Lake Erie and enormous snowstorms blanket the area. It was below zero; the snow drifts were high. Aunt Johnetta met my plane in Buffalo, and the blinding snow pelted our windshield as we followed the tracks on the highway at almost walking pace. Aunt Johnetta's gloved hands, wrapped around the steering wheel, guided us along the snow-packed road with the same steadiness and sureness that had led my mother back from her oblivion. Our spirits were high, and Aunt Johnetta's stories and soft laughter touched my soul, enfolding me, and I felt a certain tranquility during our journey homeward. She talked of friends and family, her five daughters and one son, and her husband, my Uncle Walter, who had died several years ago. She spoke about their travail and joy; it was a conversation of compassion and comedy about her daily life. Aunt Johnetta had no tolerance for unkind gossip and as I listened to her and watched her negotiate the treacherous road I relaxed, knowing I was safe with Aunt Johnetta. She reserved judgment about nature just as she did about people; she did not complain or fret, she simply attended to her own business and the task at hand. I thought of the plaque that had always graced her dining room wall; its bold script had spoken to us every time we had Sunday dinner at her house when we were growing up.

> *There is so much good in the worst of us,*
> *and so much bad in the best of us,*
> *that it hardly behooves any of us*
> *to talk about the rest of us.*

When the car swerved on the ice Aunt Johnetta allowed it to slide, turning her wheels ever so slightly, never slamming on the brakes. We arrived in Warren very late at night, and I would see Mother the next morning.

Mother had arranged for her gold Pontiac Firebird to be serviced. It was waiting for me in the garage of her apartment building. The small powerful car spun around on the snowy, icy roads a couple of times before I remembered how to drive in winter weather. I had learned to drive on icy roads when I was sixteen years old, and soon I was back in control. I let go of all my care of family and work in California and felt like I *was* sixteen years old when I drove up to the front of the nursing home.

I approached the entrance, located in the center of a long sunporch with windows steaming. Inside, shadowy figures moved slowly. I stamped the snow from my boots and entered through the double French doors. A gray and wrinkled man was sinking into a rocking chair next to a chaise lounge where a small remnant of a woman was smiling at me from underneath her ruffled white cap, a baby's cap. And then I saw my diminutive, white-haired mother leaning down to talk to another patient, who was straining to hear with an aid wired to his cheek. Mother was shouting to him, "My daughter will be here in a few minutes—all the way from California." Then she saw me. Her eyes were shining, one arm out-stretched as she supported herself on her crutch. She wore a navy blue dress with white collar and a jacket to match; her hair was combed carefully. I walked toward her and felt the years fall away. Her eyes were as bright as ever. "There you are!" she said, and our tears came.

Mother, who had been "put away," had organized her own release. She handed me a tablet with carefully handwritten instructions. She and my brother had discussed the feasibility of her returning to live in her apartment alone again, and as an alternative, he had invited Mother to live with him and his wife, Doris, in their home in Lexington, Kentucky. Mother knew that her strong independence had come to an end; she could no longer live alone. She would accept John's invitation and move to Kentucky.

Her lined white tablet contained a detailed list of belongings in her apartment to go with her, along with handwritten instructions as to who would be the recipient of the articles she could not take with her. She asked me to hire a mover and take care of shipping these things, and to arrange to have her furniture for her room in my brother's house sent to Lexington. She had it so well planned that it took only a few days for me to accomplish these tasks. Already she had put her apartment days behind her; she never went back to see it. She said, "That's over." It was something I could always count on with my mother; she did not dwell on those things she could do nothing about. "Go with the river," I heard so often in my life. Was it because she always lived by the river, and had learned from it? I felt my mother was the wisest woman I would ever know.

There were three days of my special leave remaining for me to drive Mother to Kentucky and then return to California. I drove to the nursing home to pick her up. Mother walked among the patients on the porch, making her rounds, with the aid of an arm crutch, saying goodbye to the men and women she had been taking care of since she had awakened from her drugged stupor. It was early in the morning; the freshness of the day heralded a new beginning, an adventure. She stepped warily on the shoveled sidewalk, placing her galoshes-shod feet one in front of the other, as I guided her to the driveway.

Mother stood erect by her car, holding onto the door as she looked all around her—toward the sky, to the trees laden with snow, up and down the street. She was quiet and hesitant, tender as a baby chick emerging from its shell. She breathed deeply and exhaled a fine cloud of warm air from her nostrils as she paused before getting into her car.

"I feel stronger than I expected, and so free."

She was bundled up in her black coat with its fur collar fastened under her chin. She adjusted the brim of her black felt hat and patted her hair into place.

"This's a new hat—never had a chance to wear it. I like it, don't you?"

"You look terrific, Mother," I said, as I helped her into her car. We were going to have a good trip.

We drove down Pennsylvania Avenue along the Allegheny River toward the turnpike, leaving behind the familiar dirty buildings of the United Refinery which was spewing smoke into the clear sky. The streets were etched with great drifts of snow, crisp and toasted with dirt and soot.

I asked Mother, "Would you like to drive past your apartment house, or go down to see the farm?"

"No, my dear," she said, "let's just drive out of town. We'll follow the river."

Inside myself I shed many tears and I was silent. Mother was leaving the place where she had spent her entire life.

View of downtown Warren from Washington Park

A Journey Home

My mother had lived comfortably in Lexington, Kentucky for about two years with my brother and his family. Recently she had been writing to me in California about a trip back to Pennsylvania to visit her old home town. She wanted to go home again during the summer. It had been in the middle of winter, 1970, when she moved from Pennsylvania to Kentucky. I always knew she dreamed of going back sometime.

The decision to drive her home to Warren, 600 miles away from Lexington, had been easy after Mother's last phone conversation with me. "My doctor—I call him my heart throb because he takes such good care of my heart—he tells me that it's all right for me to make the trip, but we should do it slowly and take two days to go and two days to return."

"He has you on a lot of medication. Does it all agree with you?" I asked.

She laughed, "Of course I take a lot of medication. That's why I'm doing so well! Dr. Myers simply said to me, 'Go, Anne; it's a journey you want and you'll be happy doing it.' He's a doctor I really like—he cares about happiness!" That had made sense to me, and with little hesitation I began thinking about which thruways we would be taking after crossing the river into Ohio and heading for Pennsylvania.

It was 1972, and I had preregistered for the summer session at Stanford to complete my Master's degree. "I have ten days before or after the summer quarter," I said. Mother was firm. "I'm sending you a check for your ticket. Please come before you start school. Those ten days before the quarter begins will be just enough time for us to have a little vacation." I welcomed her decisiveness, and also the chance to get away, and even though I sensed some urgency I asked no more questions. Instead I was captivated, full of enthusiasm, and ready to go. My three older children were self-sufficient now, and I could count on Mrs. Miller to be there for George and John.

The drone of the plane's steady engines, the music of it, and the cushion of clouds in my view helped me to distance myself from my hectic life of the last ten years, my living alone with five children, my job as a school nurse, the coping with it all. I welcomed the feeling of being free for a while, free to go back to my home town again, to go on a vacation. Thoughts of routines and responsibilities fell away.

Instead, familiar uncluttered images surfaced: the early summer green of Pennsylvania's forests, the gently moving water in the Allegheny River, the frayed swinging bridges over Conewango Creek, and the pussy willows at the brook's edge. And there was Ott's Run, deep in the woods where the white water crashed against worn rocks and played with tree roots while the wild violets, fragrant and unafraid, hung in clusters along the edges. My sister and I had slept there, scarcely a mile from our home, yet it seemed back then to be so deep in the woods, peaceful. I was ten years old and she was twelve; lying side by side, under rough blankets, we watched the stars appear. "I wonder about God," I said. "Me, too." My sister's voice was soft. In my mind, in my soul, I have returned there often. I would hike there next week.

The plane rolled onto the runway in Lexington. Humid air blanketed my face as I emerged from the plane. My brother John was at the arrival gate. His child-like smile had never forsaken him, and it was radiant now as he walked toward me with open arms. "You can't imagine how excited Mother is about your coming to take her on this trip, Mary." He said she hadn't been so happy for a long time. "She's been planning and planning about what she's going to do in Warren. Well, you know, she has definite ideas." He laughed as he talked, and I sensed his relief in my being there, to be with Mother. He was between jobs now as he made some serious career decisions.

It was dusk as we drove through the graceful blue grass country of winding roads and expansive meadows. White fences along the road and up and down the hillsides glistened as our headlights sought them out. I had come east two years ago to drive Mother down from Warren to live with John and his wife, Doris. Their daughter, Anne, had moved into a small room in the back of the house so that her grandmother could have the bedroom with the view of the broad front lawn. Their son John brought her library books and as mother said, "He's very kind; he kept me company."

Mother was seventy-nine years old then. "I like this horse country," she had said. "I'm a gambler at heart. I want Elsie and Hazel to come down to the Kentucky Derby." Elsie and Hazel were Mother's life-long friends; they had played duplicate bridge together. The way she looked at it, betting on a horse and winning, or bidding a grand slam and making it, they were the same; she said it all had to do with probability and it was fun. She had laughed at herself as she talked about it, and then as though to explain further she had said, "I need these games; keeps me alert." Over the past two years some friends had visited, but that was not enough. She wanted to go home again.

John's car swung into his driveway, stopping before the lighted doorway. Suddenly I was inside the house, hurrying to my mother. "There you are!" she greeted me in the hallway, a fine-boned, frail woman, whose voice was vibrant with warmth and a trace of mischief. Little rivulets of tears rolled over her cheeks, detouring along the deep lines of mirth and caring. No matter how long the intervals between our visits together, her face was always the same, unless, of course, one noticed the lines etched more deeply. Her firm chin never seemed to even quiver, and yet there was a pervasive gentleness in her countenance. Her strength was a constant I had always counted on.

"I knew you would come to take me on this trip, Mary," she said as I wrapped my arm around her thin shoulders. "I just knew it, and I want this to be a vacation for you, too. We're both going to have a vacation!"

Mother hoisted herself around, rotating her body with the use of her black lacquered crutch which was fitted like a sheath around her right forearm. She had ordered her special forearm crutch from a mail-order catalogue, and had Al at the upholstery shop cut it to her size and paint it black. "It's not like most crutches," she declared. "I think it looks smart. It's stylish—not an orthopedic look. I couldn't use a plain metallic crutch—it just didn't look right with most of my clothes." And she managed quite well with her "designer" crutch as she limped back to the kitchen with Doris. Doris pulled off her apron and announced that dinner was ready.

"I don't think I'll be around much longer," Mother said as John heaped steaming mashed potatoes onto the plate in front of her. Her words remained suspended in the air like bubbles, floating to the ground, almost ready to burst. John and I responded, speaking at the same time, a chorus, "Oh, Mother, don't say that. Of course you will."

John's silver ladle dripped smooth gravy over her mound of potatoes. "You always manage to overcome everything, Mother," he said.

"That's right!" Mother said as she looked across the table at me, seeming to speak from depths beyond her wrinkled brow. Almost always I had honored that "knowing" look. It had made me stop and think more clearly, but this time I denied her message. I was relieved when she changed the subject. "Your mashed potatoes are very smooth, no lumps, John David."

After dinner, seated in a straight chair in the living room, Mother outlined her plans. "I want this trip to be simple and easy for you, Mary. I mainly want to see my old friends—not just my party friends but my good old friends like Verna and Art Shearer, and Elsie Branch, and the Johnsons who lived just up the road in Pleasant Township. They were all so good to me when Carl was ill, you know, and the snow plows didn't come down to our driveway. After Carl had his leg amputated Art did everything for him."

Her crutch fell to the floor, and as I reached to retrieve it she said, "Leave it be. I don't need it while I'm sitting." She was in charge, and she continued, "And I

want to take the Swiss cousins out to lunch down at the
Deerhead Inn. In Warren I just want to stay at the Laurel
Motel, not be a bother to anyone. It's just across the river
from the farm. It's comfortable and I'll feel at home
there. And I want to call Marie McGarry. She always
loves to go—just call Marie and she's ready to drive to
Jamestown or Frewsburg for lunch. You know, Mary, it's
just the simple things that are important." She sighed,
tried to adjust herself in her chair so that she was more
upright, so she could catch her breath. I reached out as
though to help her. "Oh, no, I'm all right." She paused.
"I remember my friends whom I could count on." Then
Mother looked at me intently, and said again, "And,
Mary, I want, I really do want this to be a special vacation for you." Mother had a reliable trait of saying what
she meant and meaning what she said, and I loved being
with her. I was already having fun. She understood how
demanding my life had been since my husband Norm
died of a heart attack when our children were ages two
to twelve. My own father, Tom, had died when he was
thirty-eight years old, leaving Mother with four young
children. We both knew how critical it was for me to finish my Master's degree at Stanford; I needed that step up
on the faculty salary schedule. John had told me that
Mother had sent him to the bank to withdraw some
money for our trip. "Mary and I are going in style."

   After dinner Mother went to her room to put some
final items in her suitcase. I could hear her opening and

closing drawers. I poked my head in the doorway to see if I could help her with anything. "Oh, no," she said, "I've just been cleaning my drawers. I don't like to leave things in a mess." Her wastebasket was overflowing. She said, "Come on in: I want you to see how I carry my money. I like to have it where I know where it is all the time, where I can *feel* it." She unbuttoned the front of her dress and drew out a white sock carefully rolled into a small bundle. It had been lodging in her brassiere in the crevice of her bosom. Unrolling the sock she removed from its toe a roll of $100 bills. "Here," she said, "I want you to have a few of these just to get started tomorrow." I accepted the bills and we both laughed, like children in a candy store.

As I left her room she said, "We're leaving very early; you'd better get some sleep."

I did sleep well. I had stopped worrying about Mother's health or money or anything. She had mesmerized me; I had forgotten about her heart condition.

Early the next morning we prepared to leave—not even a cup of coffee—just hushed goodbyes to John and Doris, still in their nightclothes. Doris hastened to review with me Mother's medications. "Remember the diuretic, it's three times a day, but the Digitalis is only in the morning. She takes the potassium with her meals. And she knows about the little red ones."

"I know about all of them, Doris. For heaven's sake, we're going on vacation!" Mother said impatiently. But then she softened her voice. "Thank you, dear, for reminding Mary again. I do have a way of forgetting these things."

We walked down the front walk, Mother's black crutch striking the brick firmly, moving her small body forward with increasing momentum. She easily dropped into the passenger seat of her low, gold Firebird. John fastened her seat belt while I buckled myself in.

We were on our way to Pennsylvania. We tooled along in the compact car as though we had not a care in the world. Mother loved her little Pontiac. It had only 5000 miles on it when her doctor told her she could not drive it anymore because of her congestive heart failure. She checked the air vents and took the map out of the glove compartment. Carefully she gave me the directions to the thruway.

When I think of peak experiences in my life, I always remember those first few hours, just two gals off on a trip to the home town. I noticed Mother watching my every move. She seemed to be wishing she were driving her own car. But she gradually relaxed, saying, "Oh, well, you're a good driver; I'll just sit here and enjoy it." I glanced over to see her fine lively fingers seeking our place on the map. I had always loved her hands, whether they were caressing the piano keys, digging in the earth transplanting her perennials, holding firmly onto bridge cards, or simply resting in her lap. They were wonderfully expressive, sensitive, nimble hands, and I always felt love in their touch. Holding her head erect, she leaned forward, looking ahead, determined not to miss a sight. She sighed, relaxed, and looked at me with a confident smile. "I'll continue to check the map. If you get lost I'll be able to tell you where you went wrong, but I'll try to prevent it also. My eyes are good, you know—I can still thread a needle, and I can see this small print on the map." I heard her laughing.

We crossed the river, which took us through Cincinnati, and soon we were on the turnpike passing out of the city on the flat plains of the Ohio valley. It was a quiet ride, interrupted by Mother's occasional "You're driving too fast." She spent the next several hours asking questions, and getting caught up with all of my children. She wanted to know how my son, sixteen-year-old George, was doing since his illness; a star tennis player, he had been bedridden for months when he was fourteen years old with acutely swollen joints. The diagnosis was still in question. One by one I told her of everyone's latest achievement or disappointment. Mother listened intently and suddenly said, "Is there room in your house for me to live there? I think I would fit in pretty well, Mary." Her voice was matter of fact, and I felt a stillness as I glanced over at her hands, folded quietly in her lap. She had never indicated that she wanted to live in California, yet I responded as though we had already talked about it.

"Of course, Mother, I like that idea," I said and went on to explain that we could easily arrange for her to live with us. Norm and Peter were in college, and we did have more room now. My daughter, Mary, would like having her grandmother at our house. As we talked about how life would be for her in California we both gradually embraced the idea. Mother did not like to fly, but she had traveled to California on the train ten years ago. She would come on the train again after I returned to California. Now it was a fact. She would move to California.

"I like to have something to look forward to—all of my life I have welcomed the changes. I can just see myself living with your family. I'd like that." And I started making the same plans. I thought for a minute that this conversation was affirming something that was going to happen, but then I knew it was not. I put the thought aside to think about it later. It seemed as though we were talking about an idea whose time would not come. Mother was explaining, "I'm happy at John's house, but now he's planning to change engineering jobs and move to Louisville. He travels a lot and everyone in the family is busy. I seem to spend more and more time in my room. I love to read, you know. Oh, don't misunderstand me, Mary; John and Doris and the children are wonderful to me. In fact, Doris is like my best friend. She was my greatest support for this trip. She knew I was restless."

We were both gratified when we saw the Holiday Inn sign that we had been looking for. Our room was standard and comfortable. It was a new motel with an attractive restaurant that seemed to be adequate for our evening meal. However, I suggested room service because Mother seemed weary after the day's travel. But Mother said, "No, I'm fine. I want to freshen up and go into that dining room and have a proper dinner—and I can eat anything as long as it doesn't have too much salt. We're on vacation—you and I." A hint of mischief awakened in her face, reviving me, and I was caught up in her spirit of having a good time. How she could create a lightness! I was momentarily lured back to those days of Mother dancing around the kitchen with a glass of water on her head, spilling nary a drop. I was a little girl who loved her mother's play.

Seated at the table Mother called the waiter over. "We want two Tom Collinses, but please serve mine without salt." The waiter smiled at Mother and refrained from telling her that a Tom Collins does not have salt. "I like a good drink," she said, "but I could never drink that Kentucky bourbon." As we talked and remembered old times she focused on her life with her father and her early days in school. "My father was the one who checked the ice before we skated down the river to school. I was the fastest skater," she boasted, as she cocked her head with a sideways glance toward me, "and my father always told everyone about that." She would continue to talk about her father a lot on this trip. "He was the happiest person I ever knew. He never had an enemy, and he possessed a kindness that was known to everyone in Gladerun. He was a quiet man—didn't like gossip at all. 'Stop analyzing,' he'd say. 'Just let it be.'"

That evening in our room we prepared for bed. Mother had taken all her medications when she turned to me with two red capsules in the palm of her hand. "One for you and one for me," she said, as she placed a Seconal in my hand. "Oh, Mother," I protested, "I never take sleeping pills." She ignored me. "Well, tonight I want you to take one. This has been a difficult two days for you, just flying in from California, and now this long drive all day. Get a good night's sleep!" And it was true; I never took sleeping pills. In fact, I detested the idea of "reds," as the drug culture in my high school called them. But now I was completely mesmerized and I was tired. I did need a good night's sleep, and this *was* my mother. It had been the first time I had really had a chance to talk with her so intimately for more than two years. I accepted her Seconal, swallowed it with some water, and went to sleep.

The next morning as we prepared to leave the motel Mother said, "This's the way I like to travel, get a good start before breakfast and stop later for a hot cup of coffee." She said she had a good night. I carefully laid out her medications for the day. She was in excellent spirits and so was I. It was good to have just conked out for the night. Mother hesitated as she steadied herself at the door of our room. "I want you to leave a twenty dollar tip for the little maid—she was very good to me while you were down at the cashier's. She buttoned the back of my dress when I couldn't reach." She thought about that for a second and added, "She's working to support her family; she has three little children." (I remembered driving with my mother when I was ten years old up to the Rosewells who lived outside of town in a sprawling shack—formerly an old chicken coop. Her noisy Essex coupe bounced over the ruts in the frozen dirt road. When we stopped in front of their home the children flocked out to carry the bushel basket of bread and canned vegetables through the narrow door. Mrs. Rosewell and my mother hugged each other and laughed.)

"Let's have a good breakfast this morning," Mother said. "We have time. We're more than halfway there." After a second cup of coffee we left the inn and merged onto the Pennsylvania turnpike to join the stream of morning traffic. Periodically we came to toll gates and had to stop to pay fees to continue on. The Pennsylvania turnpike is scenic as it weaves in and out of foothills with wooded areas coming close to the roadway. But the speed is intense and the traffic shatters your nerves just as on California freeways. Mother became impatient. "I've never liked these big highways. Cars sound like they're going to run right over you. I'll look at this map to see if I can find where Route 8 goes up over the old Franklin Hill road." Mother sat quietly for the next hour or so, checking the map and then road signs. Suddenly, her voice was excited as she said, "Take the next exit, Mary, and we'll go up the hill. I found Route 8."

The off-ramp took us under the thruway and the road curved away from the hum of heavy traffic, winding up a narrow two-lane road, a black ribbon with a yellow line down the middle, wrapped around the mountain. We would not be passing other cars. The road was curving all the way up Franklin Hill, with yellow arrows at every bend guiding us. As small frame houses rose and fell among the green hills Mother was delighted. "I like to see people's clothes hanging on the clothesline." Her Firebird purred along at a comfortable speed and Mother remarked, "I remember that you had a good car if you could get up this hill in second gear." I felt the quiet in her voice. These were comfortable, familiar foothills. Always these Allegheny mountains, heavily forested, lush and close, invited me in, into the woods of nurturing and peace. Retreating to the High Sierras of California was for me more awesome, inspiring in a grander way. This was coming home.

Our pace was quieter now; it was peaceful as I slowed down behind farmers' trucks and other cars. "We're not in a hurry," Mother reminded me, "and it's beautiful going up the mountain." Our route would take us down through Grand Valley and eventually along the Allegheny River. Mother had her window open part way and the warm breezes filled the car with clear air, fragrant with the scent of the pine trees and honeysuckle of the State Forest. She dropped off to sleep for the first time.

"There's the river!" I could not resist awakening Mother. She was alert in an instant. "Oh, Mary, what good time you've made." The highway loomed ahead, arching over the Pennsylvania Railroad tracks; we were approaching the outskirts of Warren. "It all looks the same—it looks good." Mother sighed. She reached out and patted my hand as it rested on the steering wheel.

They expected us at the Laurel Motel. Mother admitted that she was tired and happy to go to bed. "You can order room service this evening for me, but you go down to the cafe. The food is good."

And then she began to hold court. She was a little queen. She spent her first days resting while her friends came to see her in her motel room. And there were many friends who came—old and young, frivolous and serious, bridge players, actors and actresses from the Players' Club. (Mother had been a star in some of their musical productions. Her voice had perfect pitch and with her superb presence on stage she had prompted standing ovations.)

They kept coming: Joe, the vegetable man from the Atlantic and Pacific grocery store, who was also a bridge player; her old doctor; and her undertaker friend, Leo Gibson.

"Say, Anne, do you want to go over to the cemetery to take flowers to Tom's and Carl's graves?" Leo asked.

"No, I don't," she replied. "I'm too close to being planted there myself. I'll stay away a while longer."

We all laughed with her. I remembered the day several years ago when Carl was buried. Mother had told Leo, "When I die you can put me next to Tom where there is already a headstone for me, but slant me a little bit up the hill toward Carl where he is in his family's plot."

One night I had dinner with two high school classmates while Aunt Johnetta stayed with Mother. "Go visit Marcia and Barbara; remember, this is your vacation too." I had a nostalgic evening and when I arrived in our motel room, Mother said, "I haven't laughed so much in months, and Johnetta cut my toenails and gave me a manicure. And everyone's happy, Mary, that I'm planning to move to California to live with you."

Now her plan to live with my family seemed to be a reality, and yet I still felt that it would not happen. Then Kay Shearer, Verna's daughter, called to say that she would be happy to drive Mother back to Kentucky and help her get ready to go to California. Mother was feeling anxious about my having enough time to get back to summer school at Stanford.

"You can go back to California from here," she said. "You don't need to make that drive, dear, to Kentucky."

"Nonsense," I told her, "I plan to take you back to John's myself. It's part of our vacation." And she seemed to accept that fact.

Four of the Swiss cousins joined us for the luncheon at the Deerhead Inn down on the Tidioute Road.

Mother dressed up for the occasion; she wore her new hat and a special suit she had brought along for this luncheon. She walked into the inn slowly, her black crutch secured around her right forearm, and her firm chin jutted out almost ahead of her. As soon as she reached the foyer of the inn, the owner and waitresses gave her a cheer. "Welcome home, Anne." She hesitated for a moment, responding with a gentle smile and eyes sparkling as though on center stage. "You remember me. I knew you would, and I've waited for this. Thank you, everyone." I felt my own tears and happiness, a sense of peace, as she settled into the chair at the head of the table. She was closing a chapter.

We had two more days in Warren when the rains came. It rained constantly for almost twenty-four hours, and there was a flood warning. Mother again urged me to allow someone else to drive her back to Kentucky when the weather cleared. Miraculously, the day we planned to leave the sun came out and the waters receded. We left early in the morning, still on schedule.

"We did it, Mary, and please know how happy I've been to be home again. And you had a good time, too, didn't you?"

She was right. I had found the violets growing calmly along the water's edge at Ott Run. I had taken a picture with my Sureshot camera for my sister. My concentration came back to my driving. I realized I had been in more than one world on this journey. Most of the time I had been concentrating on the task of driving the car, trying to flow with the constant stream of traffic, and trying to make good time. While focused on the driving, I listened to my mother and felt a constant gnawing anxiety inside, eating away at my sense of security. And although concern about my family in California was always with me, the present moments with my mother seemed to have a gravity I could not dispel. I refused to acknowledge or even to identify the feeling. It was just there as I heard Mother's stories about simple truths in her life. Some tales I had heard before, while others seemed to just flow as fresh water from her own fountain of youth, precious memories that she wanted to share with me. I listened intently; I needed to hear everything she said.

"I want you to know my father, Mary, and that's why I keep telling you about him." Her father, John Gander, had come to the United States from Switzerland when he was nineteen years old with his older brother, Jacob, twenty years old. They were the oldest sons in a family of ten children, and it was a matter of economics that required them to leave their homeland near Brienz where the family had a dairy farm. There was not enough food to feed all the family, and they had traveled to this country, where they also engaged in the dairy farming business. She completed the portrait of her father which she had started to sketch on the first day of our trip. I learned that he had possessed an uncommon capacity for giving love. "I just wanted you to know," Mother said.

Driving back to Kentucky seemed almost anticlimactic. Mother dropped off to sleep, and I felt alone with the hum of the motor. We had gone halfway and stopped again at the Holiday Inn. This time Mother did not offer me a Seconal. She seemed preoccupied. She had developed a slight cough and decided to have room service for dinner. But the next morning she was walking around the room very early, anxious to get going again.

That last day we were looking for a little place to have lunch. Mother suggested, "Why don't you take the next exit, and maybe we can find a small lunchroom that will have some potato soup. I'd just love a bowl of potato soup." I remembered those lean years when our whole meal was a bowl of potato soup, and bread. Bread at four cents a loaf! I drove into a roadside restaurant that had a sign describing the meals, *Homemade Soup and Sandwiches.* Mother adjusted her hat, drawing wisps of white hair behind her ear. I noticed her hat was rather askew but did not bother to tell her. We were both travel-worn by now.

The waitress smiled when Mother said, "I'll have a bowl of potato soup." We were sitting at a luncheon bar. The heavy white steaming soup was ladled out before our eyes. "There you are, honey; it was waiting for you." Mother said, "Thank you," picked up her soup spoon, nodded and smiled, as though she had planned ahead for this perfect meal.

When we left the lunchroom Mother seemed to be in a hurry. Her crutch stirred the dust on the dirt driveway as she opened the door on the driver's side of the car. As she started to get in I said, "Mother, are you planning to drive?" She stopped, took notice of where she was, and laughed. "You know, I've always liked being in the driver's seat!"

As the sun slipped away I felt relieved that we had almost reached our destination. The dusk fell softly and seemed to settle inside of me, a weariness that comes at the end of a long journey or after a busy day. Mother was now silent most of the time. Every once in awhile she asked me if I was sure I was on the right road. "Oh, I'm sorry, dear; you've done such a good driving job—I don't mean to sound critical." Mother usually did not apologize for what she said because she usually meant what she said, and she would not believe it needed apology. I turned on the headlights as Mother sat straighter in her seat to look out the window. "Now I think I can be of some help to you," she said as the green and white signs numbering the exits of Lexington appeared on the side of the highway. "John David always takes the third exit." I slowed down, preparing to turn off.

I was negotiating the curve of the exit when I heard a muffled sound, then a slight clicking noise. I looked over to see Mother slumped over on her seat belt, limp and still like a rag doll. She made a barely audible sigh. I accelerated and drove around the curve of the ramp. A Shell gas station was brightly lighted at the first turn off the exit. Our car stopped at one side of the station, away from the yellow pumps. I reached for Mother's pulse and feeling nothing, I jumped out and ran around to the other side of the car, unbuckled her seat belt, and with frantic fingers forced the knob that lowered the back of her seat. As she rolled toward me, I cradled Mother in my arms, holding her head with my hands on both sides of her face so that I could breathe air into her lungs. Silence settled around me, a dim light from the corner of the station caused a pale glow over her hands folded in her lap, and I knew my mother was not there anymore.

I felt a hand on my shoulder. As I stood up, the yellow-shirted station attendant was holding the car door wide, asking if he could help me.

"I called the ambulance," he said. I could not speak. I heard the siren getting closer. I shivered in the summer night, and the coldness in my stomach moved into every part of me. Had I made a fatal error to take Mother on this journey? Looking up into the sky—it was dark—I felt lost. A man from the ambulance told me what I already knew—that Mother was dead.

My fingers were numb as I dialed the telephone in the musty dark booth. There was no answer at my brother's house. He and his family had not yet returned from their trip to Rochester, New York and Harrisburg, Pennsylvania where he had gone for a number of job interviews. I dialed my sister Ginny's number in Vermont. When I heard her voice I began crying and talking at the same time. "I should have known better. Mother was not strong enough to take a trip!"

And then my sister said, "Mary, Mary, don't you realize that you helped her do exactly what she set out to do?" Her calm voice continued. "Mother once said that if she ever got to the point in her life where she felt she was 'just hanging on a hook in someone's closet' she'd climb the highest mountain until she dropped. Mary! You helped Mother climb her mountain!"

I walked back to Mother's little gold Pontiac, which seemed to glow under the station light. I slid in behind the wheel. Her perky colorful hat lay on the passenger's seat. Alongside was a shiny black crutch. I could still see her trying to get into the driver's seat. I could still hear her saying, "Let's go up the old Franklin Hill Road." I felt her tenderness, and as I drove away from the station I saw the sign, *Mother's Shell Station*. It was owned by Mr. and Mrs. William Mother.

It would be some time before I could accept Ginny's reassurance that I had helped Mother climb her mountain.

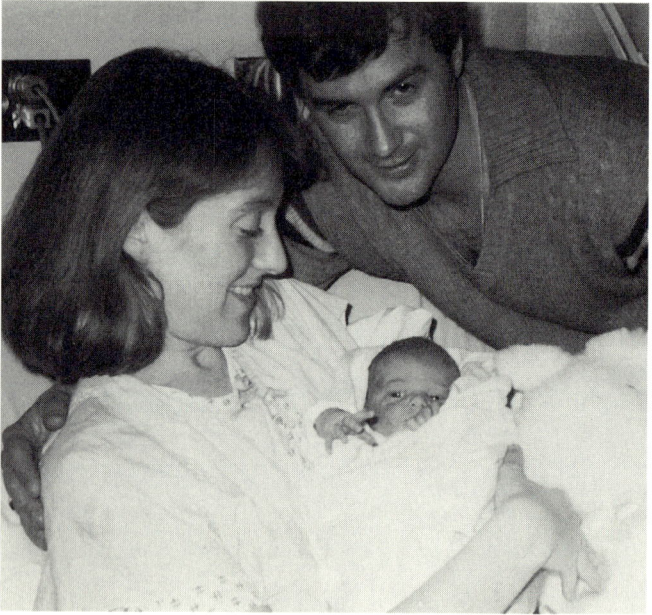

Mary and Richard with Genny

A New Birth

It was almost like being invited to a party—and then it actually turned out that way—a family party. My daughter, Mary, and her husband, Richard, asked me to be present while their baby was being born. They had been going to childbirth classes together and planned to use the alternative birth room at Stanford Hospital for the delivery.

Their invitation evoked a variety of feelings within me as I began visualizing what it might be like to attend the birth of my grandchild. I had delivered each of my five babies in a standard hospital delivery room with glaring bright lights, on a hard metal table, stirrups attached, and forbidding machines lining the walls. I asked myself if I wanted to be in the room while my daughter was going through this crisis of birth. Would I be of any help? Could I stand it?

Mary said, "Mom, we really hope you'll be there." She continued in a festive spirit, "Peter is coming, and

John says he'll fly home." It was hard to believe that she had invited her brothers. "How is that possible? I mean, so many people in the delivery room. Will they allow us all to be there?"

"It's O.K., Mom, it's just like a regular room at the hospital, and Dr. Shefren says I can have anyone in the family. Anyone who wants to come." I told her that I was pleased that they invited me, and I would let her know. But she persisted. "Richard and I have been going to our Lamaze classes and we're glad we have this choice. We really want you to come."

"All right, dear, if that's what you both want, I'll be there," I said, and hung up the receiver, feeling somewhat unsure. I thought about my daughter and the real facts of giving birth. Wouldn't it be better, easier at least, not to be at her delivery but instead to wait nearby until after the birth and then enjoy the peace of the new mother in the clean room with the pink baby? After all, that is the way it had been when I had my babies. Even their father was not present.

Sitting at my kitchen table after Mary's invitation, I thought about the hours before my first baby was born. I was alone with the doctor and nurse in the modern "safe" world where they drugged mothers well—twilight sleep, spinal anaesthesia, gas, and ether—doctors take your choice. They struggled with me in my stupefied state to position me on my hands and knees so that the doctor could pierce my spinal column with a needle and numb my entire lower body. I felt like I was far away, disconnected from my being, my legs heavy with paralysis. Through a cloudy veil I sensed my baby being pulled out of my body. My first son was removed from my uterus with great forceps; a sensation not unlike having a molar extracted from a jaw numbed by novocaine.

It was not until my third pregnancy that I was allowed to have a baby in a more natural way, that I actually had a choice. I had read Grantley Dick Read's new book *Childbirth Without Fear* and found a doctor who was a believer in this method. It was a notable improvement, but my husband was still excluded, and the lights still bright and the table still metal. It crossed my mind, if Norm were alive today, he would be invited to the party.

The delivery of my first baby was particularly traumatic because I had always anticipated that when I had a baby it would be a natural event similar to the births I had attended as a young public health nurse in Boston.

❧

Mothers in the crowded tenements of Boston delivered their babies at home, without medication, with the aid of a Community Health Association nurse and a third-year Harvard medical student. What unforgettable experiences we had! The miracle of life in Scollay

Square, the North West End, East Boston, and the South End—those memories would linger forever:

- little children whisked off to a neighboring flat
- newspaper pads, made of pieces of old sheets sewn together over layers of newspapers
- two snaps and a pair of scissors, boiling in a basin on a kerosene stove
- black rubber aprons
- wet, sterile rubber gloves on scrubbed hands
- sterile gauze sponges and a cord tie on the bedside table
- a single light bulb hanging from the ceiling
- the mother, center stage, lying across the bed, clutching and tugging on towels secured to the opposite side of the bed
- a rush of water splashing into a basin on a wooden floor
- the nervous, unshaven father, with his hand on her brow

The atmosphere in the cramped room was tense and dramatic and loving. Sometimes the medical student and I spent all day and night in the home during the mother's labor.

Finally the climax as the mother delivered her baby, groans and grunts giving way to joy and laughter. Often the baby was named for the nurse or medical student in appreciation of our being there. We celebrated with food and drink, especially the hungry mother, basking in the sheer pleasure of accomplishment.

I did not have that choice; modern medicine during the late forties and early fifties held the option of natural childbirth in low regard. Even with my experience of home deliveries I did not feel free to question the established medical practice. Home deliveries and natural childbirth were mainly for the poor, or they were shunned as the domain of midwives who were not considered legitimate professionals—at least not in urban areas.

Instead, I was privileged; we had insurance. But I was alone, drugged, and powerless—in fact, absent it seemed. "Thank God for caudals (spinal anaesthesia)," said my husband after our first baby was born, but he did not have the slightest idea what had gone on in the delivery room. He was on the golf course, then at home, and finally in the waiting room during my labor and delivery.

❦

Several weeks later Mary called at midnight; it was the week she expected to have her baby. She and Richard were living in San Francisco, and her voice seemed far away. "I'm really scared, Mom; my water just broke. Dr. Shefren told us we could wait and come down to the hospital tomorrow morning, but I think we'll come down to Palo Alto tonight."

"That's good; come down now and stay here tonight," I said. Richard's voice was excited. "We'll be right down. It's raining and I know I'll feel better being closer to the hospital!"

At 2 A.M. the phone rang. "We decided to stop at the hospital." Richard seemed calmer. "Mary's having contractions every five minutes. We talked with the doctor again and he'll be here at six o'clock this morning so why don't you come early too?"

Driving to the hospital at 6 A.M., I thought about my only daughter, bracing myself, yet amused that she had already called her four brothers; she wanted everyone in the family to be tuned in to the arrival of her baby. Gradually my own anxiety diminished, replaced with the anticipation of a totally new and wonderful experience. Mary was right; we all cared and we all wanted to be involved in some way. My pace quickened as I ran up the escalator in the hospital, the moving steps sliding away as I stepped on the firm second floor; I was on my way to be with my daughter for the birth of her baby.

I opened the door and saw a comfortable bedroom with easy chairs, pictures on the walls, draperies, flowers, and lamps. The only sign of anything medical was a table with a few packages of gauze sponges and an ordinary hospital bed.

Mary and Richard were in a corner of the room and it appeared as though they were dancing, swaying together and breathing in a rhythm as to music. I found myself beginning to sway with them. Gradually the contraction was spent and Mary took a deep breath.

"Hi, Mom, we're getting into the second stage of labor—Dr. Shefren thinks the baby will be born in a few hours." She laughed, saying, "The most frustrating thing about this is I can't find time to talk; my contractions just keep coming and we have to breathe!"

Dr. Shefren had entered the room behind me and had also observed their breathing together. He smiled and nodded his head, obviously impressed. "You're both doing exceptionally well," he said. (I felt a glow inside— a great respect for my daughter—and in those next few hours this respect would grow even greater and I would know her marvelous strength and courage.) Richard was a total help-mate, a dancing partner, and implicit in his being there was a sense of harmony. I was happy they had invited me.

Mary and Richard continued their breathing and humming together, and Mary in her labored voice between contractions said, "Oh, Mom, I called Peter after we got here. He's coming over this morning—he said he'd stay in touch, be in and out until the baby is born. And John's flying up on the noon plane from Newport Beach. I guess Norm and George will have to come later from San Diego, but isn't this great?—Oh, here comes another one!"

It occurred to me that Mary and Richard were really planning a party but they didn't know yet what was in store for them. At the same time I realized that they were handling the progressive intensity of Mary's labor with unusual perseverance and certainly admirable fortitude. I could see that they were tackling a difficult task together and intended to see it through. I needed to let go of my own reoccurring fear; I needed to remember being with Angela when she delivered her baby named Mary, at 240 Paris Street in East Boston in 1944. And here with my daughter I was constantly aware of my privilege to be present. Gradually I felt a clearing inside myself, a letting go of my own drugged, powerless experiences of birth; my fear was replaced by a sense of peace and love flowing freely as I participated in the delivery of my daughter's first baby.

Shortly after noontime Dr. Shefren came in to check the progress of labor. He conferred with Liz, the nurse, who had been monitoring Mary's contractions and dilatation of the cervix periodically. He examined Mary, turned to Liz, and said, "You can bring in the baby's crib, Liz." And to Mary and Richard he said, "I'm going to change my clothes now. It won't be long before your baby's here."

Everything had speeded up. Now I was wondering if Mary was really going to have her baby right in this room. After all, we were in a hospital. Didn't they have to take her to a delivery room? I asked Dr. Shefren, "Are you going to deliver the baby right in that bed?"

"Oh, yes," he said very matter-of-factly, "and quite soon" were his words as he left the room.

"The waves are getting bigger," Mary said, her hair damp and stringy, her face becoming flushed and blotchy at the height of each powerful surge.

"Here comes one, Richard, hold on; I want to get the most out of this one." They braced themselves with each others' arms. Liz helped Mary lie down on the bed. Beads of moisture fell from Richard's forehead, and Mary for the first time appeared to be a bit desperate. "My lower back hurts so much, Mom; please hold that pillow and hot water bottle against it as hard as you can."

Thank heavens, I sighed to myself. Finally I had something to do. I could not just sit, nor could I just stand there watching; I slid the hot water bottle under her back and held it as steadily as possible.

Dr. Shefren was ready, white coat and scrubbed hands. He examined Mary and checked the fetal heartbeat. Richard was on one side of the bed helping Mary brace herself. I was on the other side continuing to hold the pillow and hot water bottle firmly against her lower back. The doctor sat down gently, quietly on the edge of the bed, pulling on light tan sterile gloves which he had removed from the black bag on the chair beside the bed. Liz laid a sterile sheet before him on the bed. He carefully examined each sterile instrument as he removed the wrappings and placed two stainless steel clamps and one pair of shiny scissors on the white cloth. I thought of a picnic.

Mary was pushing, the baby's head emerged, guided by the doctor's skillful hands, and he gently ran his fingers around the baby's neck, feeling for the cord that might be there. It was, and he lifted the cord smoothly over the baby's head, and in a quiet voice, he told Mary that with her next contraction she would deliver her baby. Genevieve slipped into this world, into Dr. Shefren's hands, and as he held her up for all to see her better, she proclaimed her arrival with a hearty cry. He placed her on Mary's abdomen, and we all sighed in unison as we watched the pink and crying baby girl take her first breaths. Dr. Shefren clamped the cord in two places, the bright clamps gleaming side by side, and then he said to Richard, handing him the scissors, "Now you can cut the cord." Unable to believe what he heard, Richard asked, "Me?" "Yes, you can't miss." Pointing to the space between the two clamps, the doctor said, "Right there."

Richard's outstretched hand accepted the scissors, and carefully he cut the cord. Liz tied the cord, applied the sterile dressing, and wrapped the squirming baby in a blanket before placing her in Mary's arms.

There was a knock on the door while Dr. Shefren was delivering the placenta, and John walked in followed by Peter. John, always proper, Brooks Brothers suit, long-stemmed red roses in one hand and a box of cigars in the other, hesitated in the doorway. Peter, his older brother, had been in earlier and was much at ease, having been present at the births of his three babies. This morning he enjoyed "just being an uncle." When John saw the blood he started backing out of the room. "Oh, Mary, I'm sorry; I've come too soon."

"Oh, no," said Dr. Shefren, "you're just in time, John; come on in." Mary encouraged him further. "Oh, yes, John, don't you want to see my placenta?" Still backing away, half-smiling, John responded, "No, Mary, I don't think I want to see your placenta. I'll pass."

Dr. Shefren, a part of our family by now, held up the placenta, dangling from the umbilical cord. "Well, here it is, John."

Laughter took over as John found himself in a familiar role as the youngest member of our family. He was accustomed to the teasing from his older brothers, and he relaxed as Dr. Shefren motioned him into the room to see the baby in Mary's arms. We took turns holding the baby as Liz removed the soiled linen.

Mary, now refreshed, lying back, comfortable, with the bed slightly raised, said to Dr. Shefren, in fact to all of us, "You know, that was the hardest thing I've ever done." And Dr. Shefren agreed. "Yes, Mary," he said very soberly, "and this is a lesson you've learned about life. Remember this strength and courage you have—it will help you in many ways, many times." The magic of that moment was interrupted but not diminished by Peter, who was holding the baby. "Mary, you should nurse her.

She wants to eat right now; really, I'm not kidding; look at her." Genny was vigorously sucking her fingers. Mary with a soft laugh responded, "I'm too tired." And Richard chimed in, "So am I."

A tray of blueberry muffins arrived along with the aroma of a pot of coffee. "I'm starved," Mary said. "Let's eat." The party was in full swing. Mary said afterward, "Mom, I know that Dad was in the room with us."

❦

In my mind's eye was a vivid picture: the nurse with our first-born baby, bringing Normie to my bedside so his father and I could see him, cuddle him for the first time; it was the most inspiring experience I had ever known.

And so it was with each of our new babies when Norm and I saw the miracle of life contained within a tiny, helpless infant. The delicate hands that groped aimlessly, the strong cry, the little eyes so new to this world that they hesitated to flicker open; all of these were beyond comprehension. I saw the same joy and wonderment in the eyes of Mary and Richard as they watched Genny's fingers find her mouth. And I remembered the careful gentleness of Norm's large hands when he would hold one of our babies close to his chest.

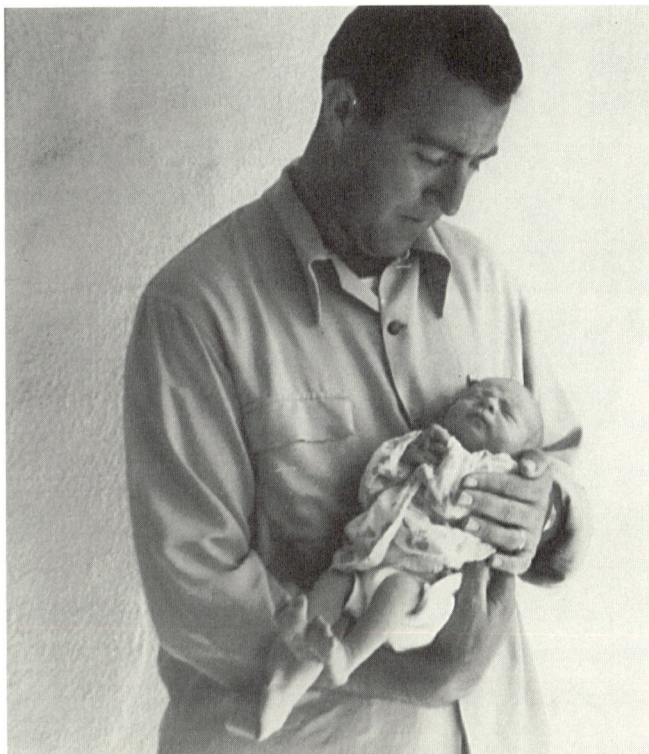

Norman, Sr. with Norman, Jr., July 1948

John, Ginny, Mary, Tom, 1946

Captain Ripley Buckingham
Army Medical Reserve Corps
Born in Brandon, Vermont, August 19, 1912
Killed in Action, Sungshan, China, August 18, 1944

Brown Babies
and Pink Babies

My deep feeling about the equality of races was reinforced when I served in the Army Nurse Corps during World War II in 1944. Thirty-five years later this clear understanding in my heart and soul came alive when one of my sons married a young black woman, a native of Trinidad. During the course of my life, my awareness of the question of disparity concerning origin and color among people had developed gradually, and concomitantly my own knowing that it was the heart, the spirit of a person that was significant, not the race or nationality.

❦

I had grown up in a wholly white world in a small town in Pennsylvania. As a child in the twenties, and without television, I was unaware of races until my sister, Ginny, and I spent one summer at our grandmother's dairy farm in Virginia. Proudly my grandmother told the story of our grandfather, Thomas George Hezakiah Wright, who served in the Confederate Army during the Civil War. "He fought under General Stonewall Jackson," she said, "and he was buried in his Confederate uniform just like he wanted to be."

The farmhouse was a weathered, two-story, sturdy structure built in 1812. In the dim downstairs hallway sat a great wooden chest, and nearby in one corner nestled several cannon balls which had been recovered by my uncles while tilling the fields. We imagined the chest contained guns and other war stuff, but no one ever opened it for us to see.

The Little Antietam Creek ran through my grandfather's 365 acres of farmland. Further north in Maryland, the Northern Virginia Army had fought in the fierce Battle of Antietam, a crucial conflict of the bloody, four-year war. There were several bullet holes in the heavy front door of the old farmhouse, which seemed shrouded in mystery and history. I wished that the wide-planked wood floors, the wide staircase, the many bedrooms, the long hallways, the wash tables with the basins and pitchers, and the round pots under the beds—I wished all of them could talk and tell me stories of the lives of those who had lived and died there. My grandmother said that there were hollow spaces between the two stories of the farmhouse. These air spaces served to keep the house cooler in the summer and warmer in the winter. She told us that during the Civil War

Confederate soldiers were concealed in those narrow spans, hiding from the Union soldiers. She also told us that earlier on, before the war, runaway slaves had found refuge in those same hiding places.

The grandmother we knew was really our step-grandmother. My grandmother, Alberta Gardner, died when she was very young, and after her death my grandfather asked his four children to select a wife for him so they would have a mother. They chose Roberta Light, a young woman who lived nearby and for whom they had great affection. He married Roberta, and he called her "Bertie," just as he had addressed my grandmother by her shortened name, "Bertie." The tombstones of both of my grandfather's wives have *Bertie Wright* inscribed on them, with different dates of birth and death. My middle name is Alberta, and I barely escaped being called "Bertie."

My father, Thomas George Wright, left home when he was fourteen years old, after his mother died and his father remarried. He was tall and lanky, mature for his age, and he found a job in Pennsylvania as a linesman for the Bell Telephone Company. My father was a handsome, industrious man, deeply respected by all who knew him; during his almost twenty-five years with Bell Telephone he worked his way up to become a foreman in the field. My knowledge of my father came from stories my mother told, and also in my vivid memory I saw his smile when he crouched down, arms held wide to catch me, as I ran down our street to meet him when he came home from work. Also in my memory is a lunch pail dangling from one hand, and I feel his other hand on my head, as he ran his fingers through my curls. During my growing up years, I believe I knew he was there and would catch me.

My father's love and high regard for the farm in Virginia where he was born were deeply embedded in his soul. He chose to return there to die when he was thirty-eight years old, terminally ill with "sugar diabetes" and "consumption." He had been a patient at the Mercy Hospital in Pittsburgh, Pennsylvania, 150 miles from our home in Warren, Pennsylvania. My mother visited him in the hospital often, but we four children, ages two, four, six, and eight years, had not seen him for many months. One of the nuns, his nurse, wrote to Mother, "Mr. Wright can talk only of his family; they are the most important thing in the world to him." She told of his desire for us all to be together on the farm in Virginia during his last days.

I recall the somber mood in our home when my mother left to go to Pittsburgh to take my father to Virginia. Uncle Gilbert, my father's half brother, came north to accompany my sister and me and our two brothers on the train trip down to the farm. I was four years old, and I remember standing at my father's bedside with Tom and Ginny while my mother held John David. My father's weak voice, from the depth of the soft pillow cradling his head, spoke to us. "You're good children, and I know you'll take care of each other and your mother." Ginny and I wore our best dresses. During those few days on the farm everyone was nice to us, showering us with toys and lots of ice cream. Skeleton thin, and travel weary, my father died a few days after arriving in Virginia. Following his death our grief-stricken family returned with his body to Pennsylvania for funeral services. He was buried in the cemetery not far from our home.

It would not be until the summer of 1930 that we would return to the farm. It was during the Great Depression, and Mother drove Ginny and me down to Virginia to leave us with our grandmother for the summer months. I was eleven and Ginny was thirteen years old. Even though the farm hardly paid for itself, our grandmother was happy to help Mother by keeping us occupied during that summer vacation. My grandmother along with two of our uncles ran the dairy farm. Hired hands helped with the milking. Two of the hired men lived in the attic over the back part of the house. Additional hired hands were "colored men" who came from outlying places to help with the milking.

One morning Ginny and I went to breakfast in our flowing beach pajamas, each a one-piece creation with a scanty halter top. They were the fashion rage that year, and we had made them ourselves, pedaling furiously on our mother's Singer sewing machine to finish them for our summer vacation. My sister's were orange and mine were pink; we felt stylish in them. But our grandmother said they were not very modest. "I don't want the men to see you in those things," she said, and waved us back upstairs to our room. We had to leave our beach pajamas in our suitcase for the remainder of our visit.

Every morning after the milking was finished we ate breakfast at the long wooden table in the kitchen with the hired men who lived in the attic, my uncles, and the two colored men. One of the colored men liked to sing hymns. "Brighten the corner where you are," he sang while we ate ham and eggs and fried potatoes and drank fresh milk with chips of ice in it. My grandmother waited on everybody, bringing broad plates loaded with freshly baked rolls. Butter, scooped out of the churn, melted into the hot bread at six o'clock in the morning, as we heaped on the strawberry jam, jam from berries we had picked the day before. Our grandmother baked bread and rolls every day before dawn.

There will forever be a vivid video in my mind's eye of my grandmother: she's in a simple faded blue dress with a wide skirt, her thin grayish-brown hair rolled into a tight knot secured with black hairpins high on the back of her head. She's sitting on a low stool in the barn, milking a cow alongside my uncles and the hired men, each beside a cow. I can see and hear the milk as the strong spurts hit the sides of the pails.

I recall the pictures, but I remember very few conversations with my grandmother. She was not a talker, except for her proud description of our grandfather in his uniform during the war. When we first arrived, she took time to tell us about the farmhouse and show us our bedroom with the pitcher and basin on the washstand, and the pot under the bed. She took us outside and led us down a narrow path, fringed with tall grass, to introduce us to the "outhouse," a small wooden structure with a swinging door that latched inside with a hook and eye bolt. On the long broad seat in this private structure, called a privy, there were two large holes, and one small hole to accommodate smaller rear ends. She showed us the outside washing place by the water pump. "You must get up early," she said. "We have breakfast at dawn." Mainly it seemed she was consumed with work: milking cows, feeding chickens, filling troughs for pigs and hogs, drawing water out of the well, washing and ironing (with a flat iron that always sat, ready and hot, on the back of the wood stove), weeding, gathering vegetables, picking fruit, cutting heads off chickens, plucking chickens, churning butter, canning, sweeping, cooking, baking. She seemed to have no time or inclination to have us help her, or to waste her time talking. And we didn't want to bother her because she was so busy.

I believe my grandmother's greatest joy and only diversion came on Sunday when she went to church and sang hymns. And she seemed the very happiest when she used the thick cream to make peach or berry ice cream on Sunday afternoons. She allowed us to help; we sprinkled salt on the ice around the cylinder in the freezer as she rotated the handle to keep it whirling. "This's the richest ice cream in the world," she said. And we knew it was.

Ginny and I enjoyed the freedom our grandmother gave us to be busy or lazy. We played in haystacks in the barnyard, and once Ginny fell through a tall one and landed on a cow's head. But mostly we explored the meadow and the woods along the shallow creek. Cedric and William, the black men, were our good friends. They helped us with Millie, the horse our grandmother had told us we could ride bareback. "She won't cause you any harm," she had said. But we were a little afraid anyway, so I asked Cedric, the one who liked to sing, "Would you help us, Cedric? Ginny and I are kind of afraid to put the bit in Millie's mouth." He laughed but then became serious. "C'mon," he said. "I need to show y'all something about Millie. She's a good horse but she's gettin' old." Ginny and I followed him as he picked up a handful of hay, kicking a stone along the path to the barn. Millie was in her stall but turned away from us as we came toward her. When Cedric offered her the hay she turned to sniff it, and she looked at him when he patted her neck and I thought she smiled. "See, girls," he said. "Just let her know you like her; y'want to take care of her."

He pulled the reins and the bit off the hook in the corner of the barn, slid the metal piece into her mouth, between her teeth, and holding the reins led Millie over to the barnyard fence. "Here you are," he said to Ginny, handing her the leather reins. "Just bring her closer to the fence, so's you can step up on the rail and swing your leg over." Ginny lost no time following directions, sitting up straight on Millie. She wore boys' overalls that Mother bought at "Monkey" Ward's. Her skinny legs, sticking out of the rolled-up pants, swung back and forth—her black tennis shoes brushing against Millie's brown coat. "See," Cedric said. "You can ride Millie anywhere as long as you're gentle with her." Ginny and I never thought of her as old; we just thought she seemed wise and graceful. We took turns straddling her sagging back as we trekked down the lane toward the creek. Ginny reached up for leaves from trees as she guided Millie, and I picked wild flowers and their foliage along the meadow path and beside the creek; we were gathering specimens for our Girl Reserve nature study project.

The summer passed quickly, and when we assembled our pressed leaves and flowers they all had names; Cedric and William had helped us identify every specimen in our collection. Ginny and I saw that their skin was darker than ours, and people called them "colored men," yet we didn't think of them as different; they were friends and helped us a lot. I believe something touched my soul that summer, and forever left its imprint. I still think of the tenderness of the "colored men" when I see a jack-in-the-pulpit, a trillium, or a violet finding its way from beneath a blanket of leaves in the woods where the sunshine filters through.

My Virginia summer raised questions in my mind about wars, about divisions in our country, and awakened in me an awareness of people of different color. We had whiled away the summer on a farm steeped with reminders of strife and violence among men in times past. Were we just marking time in the calm after the storm while we stayed with our grandmother? I had seen a newsreel in a movie house—the discord caused by the Depression, the fighting for food and jobs. I didn't understand the foreboding feeling when I first saw the film, but down on the farm the realization came to me that the world was full of strife.

Still Ginny and I waded in the waters of the creek and were refreshed. As we sloshed about in the cool water, I thought of my father as a boy, probably kicking and splashing with great vigor, and feeling the flow I felt as I stood still on mossy rocks in the shallow curve of the creek. It was the same creek that he had known, but the flowing water was always changing. The end of summer came, I had just begun my period, and I was relieved when our mother arrived to take us home to Pennsylvania.

The following school year I was consumed with the desire to study about the Civil War in my history class. I thought about the cannon balls, the bullet holes in the front door. Had that onslaught helped provide freedom for Cedric's father and grandfather? Were they freed by the soldiers who were fighting against my grandfather? Why had my grandfather helped runaway slaves escape, and yet served in the Confederate Army? As I lived in the question, I was required to memorize the Gettysburg Address. Lincoln's words "all men are created equal" crystallized the truth for me. I knew that no person intrinsically is better than another, any more than one grain of sand is better than another. And it would be during another war, World War II, that I would see that truth played out for me.

❦

In the beginning of the year 1944 the war news became more horrifying daily. My two brothers and my sister's husband were in the service, one in Europe, one in the South Pacific, and one in China. I was a graduate nurse, imbued with a sense of service; I needed to join the Army. I had no idea what joining the Army would mean. It never occurred to me that I was also giving up very personal freedom. Nevertheless, I probably would have joined up anyway because the whole world was in terrible turmoil then and individual preference was not an issue.

My first tour of duty was at Fort Knox, Kentucky in a regional hospital receiving the wounded from the European theater of war. The dearth of staff at the regional hospitals in the United States, because of the need for medical personnel overseas, necessitated twelve-hour duty—seven days a week—for the few nurses who remained after a large contingent had been shipped out. One early morning when I came off night duty, a telegram was thrust into my hand by an administrative officer. "I'm afraid it's bad news," he said. I read the shattering message from my mother. My sister's husband, Ripley, a doctor in the medical corps in China, had been killed in action. Death was touching all of us, and there seemed to be no end in sight. I heard my heart pounding as I lay on my bunk thinking of Ripley. I thought of my sister in her wedding dress less than two years ago, and cried into my pillow over her broken heart. And Ripley's mother and father? They had lost their only child. None of this made any sense. Here, in this hospital, German prisoners were helping me care for American soldiers wounded in Europe; a Japanese sniper in Sungshan, China targeted medical corps insignia on the back of Captain Ripley Buckingham's olive drab shirt; my brother Tom was in the Army in Germany; my brother John was in the South Pacific with the Army Engineers.

I did not sleep all day. Finally it was time to return to work at 7 P.M. I walked toward my station of duty, engulfed in the darkness of the early evening, and the hollow sound of my footsteps on the raised and warped wooden ramp echoed my grief. I knew my refuge was in the hospital wards where every bed cradled an injured soldier—where at least I had a job to do.

Fort Knox Regional Hospital was constructed as a cantonment, a series of long, narrow buildings extending outward from wide wooden ramps to house all the wounded soldiers, shipped from overseas. Each elongated structure had two rows of beds extending from one end to the other, accommodating fifty patients. These wards were strung out side by side and the connecting ramps seemed to run for miles. To make up for the shortage of nurses and medical corpsmen, German prisoners of war (briefly trained as medical helpers) were assigned to each ward to assist the nurse in the care of the patients. These soldiers, known as trustees, marched down from the barb-wired, fenced-in stockade on a hill behind the hospital, singing a song which was often heard on the radio those days, "Don't fence me in...just turn me loose," in robust German accents. Their good humor spilled over onto the wards as they cared for American wounded soldiers.

I was in charge of several wards and had the help of one G.I. corpsman and several German medics. Mainly my task was to give penicillin shots and change surgical dressings while supervising the care and treatment of all patients. Forever I shall remember an eighteen-year-old

German soldier named Horst. He cared for Bryant, an emaciated, critically wounded black sergeant, whose home was in Tennessee. Bryant was an inspiration to other patients with his stalwart attitude and never a complaint, yet he suffered the most. He had lain on a board for weeks, in an evacuation hospital in France, waiting to be transported to the United States to have surgery for his shattered back. Friction and pressure had destroyed the flesh at the base of his spine; a crater-like bedsore caused constant pain.

Horst was meticulous in his effort to heal Bryant, routinely lifting and turning him to bathe and dress his wounds, as though caring for a baby. The spirit of these two men from opposing armies rose above all else that was happening in the world; the caring and the gratitude, of each one for the other, helped us all through every day. The differences in color, in nationalities, were unimportant, and for myself the healthy pink flesh filling in and healing the deep wound in Bryant's back was symbolic of what really mattered. When Bryant left Fort Knox to go to a hospital nearer his home in Tennessee for surgery, Horst gave him a gift, a watercolor of the Matterhorn. Although he had created the painting in the confines of the stockade on the hill above the hospital, he had captured the pristine beauty of the mountain rising into the clouds.

One episode during my tour of duty with the Army Nurse Corps portrayed a dark side of human nature that

I had never before encountered. Nor would I ever forget the shame I felt for my commanding officer, and for
myself also, a sense of disgrace—the hypocrisy in my
return of her salute. Having completed a month of night
duty I was given a daytime assignment on the officers'
ward. One indelible day, at lunchtime, two black officers
invited me to ride in a jeep with them to the mess hall.
"Lieutenant Wright," said the tall handsome Captain
Ellington, who had told us that he was Duke Ellington's
nephew, "let's go to lunch; we'll give you a ride."
My relief nurse had just arrived so I accepted. "Thanks a
lot," I said. "I'd love it." And I meant it. Both these
officers were good friends; they were ambulatory
patients, often helping the German medics and me,
responding to patients' requests for reading material,
cigarettes, crutches, or urinals.

We climbed into the jeep. Captain Ellington sat in
the driver's seat, while Nathan, the other black officer,
patted the seat beside him. "Sit here, Lieutenant, and
hang on," he said to me. I slid in between them. We
zoomed away from the officers' ward on the far end of
the long row of hospital buildings, and skirted the entire
cantonment. As their jeep picked up speed we laughed
all the way. There were a few magic moments of freedom
for me—flashing back to high school days when one of
my friends had a convertible. We pulled up in front of
the mess hall and jumped from the jeep. I was flanked by
the two officers as we swung open the double screen

doors and entered the mess hall. I felt flushed and breath-less and well cared for, loving the attention. "We go back to our units tomorrow," Captain Ellington said, "so this's a kind of farewell." We became serious as we toasted each other with our Cokes. Hope was in the air that the war was almost over.

After lunch, back at my nurses' station, the phone rang. I answered and a voice said, "Lieutenant Wright, this is Captain Budinski; report to Colonel Pratt's office immediately! Your relief nurse has her orders; she will remain at your station 'til you return." I responded with a "Yes, Mam," and hung up the receiver, wondering why the colonel wanted to see me. I began the long walk to the administrative offices. All Fort Knox nurses were afraid of Colonel Ada M. Pratt, from Padukah, Kentucky. She was one of the highest- and longest-ranking mem-bers of the Army Nurse Corps. I hesitated outside her office, ran my hands down the sides of my uniform, hop-ing to make it look neater, readjusted my cap, then opened her door and saluted the nurse captain at the front desk. Expressionless, she returned my salute and ushered me in to report to the colonel. Colonel Pratt sat behind her desk. I thought—I shall not be afraid.

It appeared as though she had been waiting impa-tiently for me; her freckled, mottled skin reddened as I stood before her. She studied me and pushed herself up and out of her chair. She was a stocky woman about five feet tall, but she appeared taller with her brown and

white seersucker, Army regulation nurse's cap perched
on top of her coarse russet-colored hair. I stood at attention, saluted, and said, "Lieutenant Wright reporting."
She responded with a perfunctory wave of her hand and,
losing no time, said in a loud, rasping voice, "I will not
have my nurses running with niggers—do you hear?—I
will not have my nurses talking with niggers—I won't
have my nurses eating with niggers. You've disgraced us!"
With every command her pointed finger moved closer
to me. Finally she stepped back, put her hands on her hips,
and continued, "If I *ever* see you with a nigger again you'll
be sorry! Dismissed," she ordered. "Yes, Mam." I saluted,
and she touched her forehead in response.

She followed me out of her office. "Lieutenant," she
said, "turn around," and as I faced her, she looked at the
front of my sweater. "Button that top button on your
sweater, Lieutenant, and keep it buttoned!" I fumbled for
the button of my tan regulation sweater, as tears welled
up but did not spill over. I felt the heat of outrage. "Yes,
Mam," I shot back. She had given me the last lash. I
yanked my hand to my forehead. The colonel flicked me
a careless salute to dismiss me a second time. At first I
thought I could not find my way back to my station of
duty; it was as though I had had the wind knocked out
of me; I felt lifeless. Then a feeling of disgust consumed
me. Who did she think she was? How could she wear the
uniform of the U.S. Army and talk with such viciousness
about my friends—be so horrible? I walked fast, hardly

aware of my surroundings, talking out loud to myself, just putting one foot in front of the other as I hurried up the ramp toward my ward. There was nothing I could do; I was under Colonel Pratt's command. But an awareness surged inside me, a knowing that the colonel had no power over my own inner spirit, my own convictions. I would just have to survive in the service until the war was over. When I arrived on my ward I knew I could not tell my patients why the colonel called me in. It would be too painful. Just as it would be difficult to live in the Army, under orders of my superiors, and maintain my own integrity. However, a few months later the war was over and I was able to return to civilian life. The scene with Colonel Pratt would remain with me forever.

❧

Those Army days faded into the past as the years went by, but memories surfaced again when our country became involved in the Vietnam War. My oldest son was in the lottery, but his number was not called, and he did not have to join the service. The mood of his generation became increasingly rebellious as so many soldiers lost their lives in hopeless battles. It seemed the young people of the sixties were searching for truth, intent on making their own rules.

I had returned to Stanford for graduate work. Most of my classmates were the ages of my older children, and

I often shared the seminar discussions at our dinner table. I honored their generation's open-mindedness, their focus on love and truth, their tolerance of others. However, it was unexpected and somewhat of a surprise to me when my son, Peter, who had graduated from U. C. Berkeley, announced that he and Jackie Walker, his girl friend of many months, were going to be married. Jackie was a black woman whom Peter had met in San Francisco. She was born in Trinidad and had moved to Brooklyn when she was ten years old to live with her grandmother, after her mother died. She had graduated from Howard University, in Washington, D.C., and had come to California to find a job. When Peter met Jackie she was a loan officer in a bank. Recognizing her ability and proud of her ambition, Peter laughed when he said to me, "I think her goal is to be Chairman of the Board of Chase Manhattan!"

There was a part of me that knew marriage might not be easy for them. Peter and I had some long talks. I shared with him my concern about living with prejudice—how difficult it might be for them and for their children. But my own absolute belief came through clearly to me; I knew that it was not the color of skin but human caring that matters. Peter and Jackie were married, and we had a reception at our nearly all-white tennis club. It was a mixture of black and white people, including my relatives from Vancouver and Vermont and

Jackie's Aunt Merle from Brooklyn. Tennis friends of mine told me that it was the best party they had ever attended and that it was the first party they had ever been at with black people. My sister Virginia and her husband Bob danced the night away.

As I write this story I have four granddaughters. Three are Peter and Jackie's children—Siena, Angela, and Yvonna—and one is my daughter's and her husband Richard Waldron's little girl, Genevieve. Siena's middle names are Yvonne, in respect to her maternal grandmother, and Virginia, honoring her Great-aunt Virginia who was named after the state our Confederate grandfather loved so dearly. My grandchildren call me "Mama," the name Siena, my oldest grandchild, created. I have been fortunate to live in the same town where my first grandchildren were born. I was able to experience the joy of their births, and also to participate in the nurturing of our tiny premature twins while they struggled to live. Angela and Yvonna made history in the Infant Intensive Care unit at Stanford University Hospital because they were among the tiniest babies to survive there. They weighed one pound three ounces and one pound four ounces.

I remember vividly those days when Jackie, five months pregnant with twins and with very high blood pressure, was diagnosed as having toxemia of pregnancy. Suddenly she was in the hospital on complete bed rest.

Jackie would remain on bed rest for the duration of her pregnancy. Our family felt as though we were walking on a tight-rope; either Jackie might lose the babies, or we would lose Jackie with eclampsia. If Jackie's blood pressure, blood tests, or urine tests became too severely abnormal it would be necessary to deliver the babies in order to save Jackie. On the other hand, the babies need-ed at least six or seven more weeks in utero to have any chance to survive. So the course of treatment required constant evaluation, maintaining a vigil day and night.

It was difficult for Jackie to sleep in the hospital and the expense was depressing. We decided the best solution for keeping Jackie in bed and at the same time caring for two-year-old Siena would be for Jackie and Siena to stay at my house in Palo Alto. Because I had a nursing back-ground, I would be able to take Jackie's blood pressure every three hours, test her urine, and keep a daily record while she was on complete bed rest. Peter and I were relieved when Dr. McGann, their family physician at Mid-Peninsula Health Center, and Dr. Gerald Shefren, obstetrician, made the arrangements for home care. There were many ups and downs and twice test results demanded that Jackie be readmitted to the hospital for brief periods of observation. Finally, at twenty-six weeks' gestation she went into labor at my home and I rushed her to the hospital for delivery.

Jackie recovered rapidly but the struggle for the babies to survive would continue for months. At first I felt helpless and would leave the hospital in a daze questioning the possibility of babies so tiny being able to live. Certainly it would be months before they could bring the babies home, and already the minutes and the hours seemed endless. I wondered how Jackie and Peter, how all of us, could handle these long months of uncertainty.

On my way home from the hospital one day, feeling discouraged, I stopped at Stapleton's flower shop and bought two tiny gardenia plants to bring a ray of life and hope into my home and heart; they would be symbolic of my fragile granddaughters—delicate, almost transparent, miniature beings—precious flowers. The following day I received permission, as her grandmother, to sit in the Intensive Care Nursery and hold Angela. She and Yvonna were now four months old, and Yvonna was reaching her four pounds in weight which would allow her to go home. (Angela had had an ileostomy for a perforated bowel when she was one week old, weighing less than a pound. Now she weighed almost three pounds, and needed to gain more in order to be strong enough for the operation to reconnect her bowel.) I wore a gown and mask, and sat on a chair in her cubicle while the nurse laid my granddaughter in my arms. An array of fine plastic tubing trailed from a dripping bottle and metered tank and disappeared under her blanket, supplying her body with nourishment and oxygen. Although she had the weight of a feather, I felt an amazing strong presence as I held Angela for the first time. I went daily to hold my granddaughter, and my spirits soared whenever I departed, after holding her for awhile, knowing she had been comforted and strengthened.

❦

Entry in my journal: August 10, 1984

My gardenias—the purity of their whiteness, the fragrance of them filling my home, drifting into every corner. The lush green shiny leaves, tender leaves. Our little girls are hanging onto their lives in the Intensive Care Nursery. My gardenia plants have blossomed many times. I have cared for them with sunshine, water and weekly feedings. Daily I talk to them. They are thriving. At the same time Angela and Yvonna have slowly grown. Yvonna is beginning to blossom, she weighs almost four pounds. Angela, still budding, lies under bright lights with tubes in and out of her body, waiting to gain enough weight to undergo surgery to reconnect her bowel.

Entry in my journal: October 14, 1984

I went to the hospital early today to visit Angela. Peaceful was she, her beautiful little face lost in slumber caused my tears. She had always been uncomfortable following her surgery when she was one week of age, her bowels spilling onto her abdomen through an ileostomy. Today, three days after the surgery to reconnect her small intestine, she seemed to be at ease. She must have felt so disconnected. I know I did when we fed her by syringe directly into her stomach. She is learning to nipple, to take food by mouth. When I hold her she looks at me like an old soul, the way her bright eyes find mine, the way they stay fixed to mine. I think she knows me well. My gardenias flourish.

❦

Yvonna was able to go home from the hospital at four months of age, weighing four pounds, but Angela would not be strong enough to leave the hospital until she had gained more weight.

Finally, after successful surgery, Angela was discharged from the hospital. She was seven months old, weighed almost four pounds, and was beginning to take nourishment from a bottle. In the book, *A Time to Be Born, a Time to Die,* by Rasa Gustaitis and Ernle Young, "Miracle Baby" is the title of the chapter describing Angela's and Yvonna's struggle for life.

And I thought about my life, my mother's and my father's, my grandfather's, and humanity's problem of intolerance, and realized that my granddaughters are not only miracle babies because they survived but also because in them was a healing of the wound of history. My next grandchild born was Genevieve Mary Waldron, the daughter of my daughter Mary and her husband Richard. Siena, who was two when Angela and Yvonna were born, was a veteran of baby care at the age of three and one-half when Genny was born; she had supervised the nurturing of her twin sisters. Enthralled with her new cousin she reached into the bassinet to touch the soft skin of the squirming infant. "Mama, Mama," she said to me, "we have brown babies and a pink baby." Yes, I thought to myself, and I am privileged to have both. Siena's vision of reality was clear and true, not cluttered with the years of human dissonance, discrimination, and division which had created labels of black and white.

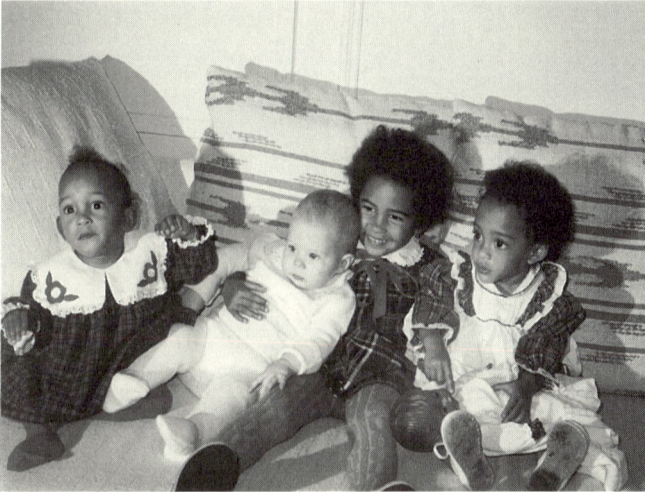

Angela, Genny, Siena, Yvonna, 1985

Dr. Loren Bensley, Mary, Dr. Warren Schaller, at
International Conference of Health Education, Paris, 1973

The Eternal Longing

A writer friend once said to me, "Mary, it seems to me you always 'celebrate the possible,'" citing a quote from poet Allen Ginsberg. Perhaps my optimistic attitude, this recognition of possibilities, explains my response when someone says to me, regarding the men in my life, "And you never married again?" It's a factual question and yet without hesitation, now in my seventies, I still respond, "No, not yet." They are surprised to hear my answer, knowing that my husband died when we were in our thirties. But I think to myself how little we change in some respects as the "bird is on the wing," and our life flies by.

When I was in nurses' training in Boston in the 1940s, the lyrics of a song in *Casablanca,* "Woman needs man and man must have his mate…that no one can deny… it's still the same old story…" struck a chord that still resonates somewhere within me. My desire for the attention of men has never wavered over the years. There was a time when I made the occasional offhand remark, "My husband died at the age of thirty-eight, and I've only been able to relate to thirty-eight-year-old men ever since"; it revealed how one can be stuck, although it is masked in humor, in an emotional rut. Finally at this stage of my life I am less flippant, more inclined to go with the flow, dealing with the reality of living alone.

However, this inexorable longing, the joy—a kind of fulfillment—of having a man in one's life, came to mind the other day while I was discussing with a seventy-two-year-old friend her flirtation with a certain gentleman whom she had met on a cruise. We sat in Talbott's Bar and Grill, giggling like school girls. "You know, Sarah," I said, "we sound like teenagers; we haven't changed that much when it comes to talking about men, about wanting a man." I went on to say, "We should be taping this conversation: it'd make a great story." No longer involved with the man she met on a cruise, Sarah was more recently kindling a relationship with a professor she had met at a modified aerobics class.

But I had asked her to meet me at Talbott's because I wanted to share with her the latest intrigue in my life concerning a man. During the week just passed, I had an encounter with a man two years older than I who had been struck by my energy and vitality when we met on a bike path. He knew me from years ago and wanted to rekindle a friendship.

"Begin at the beginning, Mary," insisted Sarah. "So you met him on a bike path, and he wanted to come to your house? What's he look like? Is he married?"

"Well, yes, he's married, but I didn't know that at first. He said, 'I'm really alone—have been married, but she's in poor health, lives with her cousin, we more or less go our own ways,' but then he changed the subject."

"Tell me," said Sarah. "What does he mean—they go their own ways—is he separated from his wife, or what?"

"I think, I sort of disregarded that marriage stuff at first, Sarah, because he kinda did, and truly it felt good to have him recall earlier days. He actually said to me, 'I should have married *you*.'"

"Go on, go on," Sarah said. "He actually said that? I want to hear more."

"Yes, he really said that—it was extraordinary the way he looked at me. It was a brisk day, his face was flushed—you know—a little December chill in the air. He looked healthy and kept saying, 'God, you look good!' Honestly, Sarah, it was very uplifting—you know what I mean?"

"I sure do—that's like that Bill—you know, the cruise guy. Well, when we were dancing, he kept saying, 'You move like a teen-ager,'" said Sarah, shaking her head and rolling her eyes. "But you know, his saying that made me dance even better!"

"That's it—unbelievable how a little positive remark makes you feel so good," I said, "and be so gullible! Well, he wanted to call on me, and asked if he could come visit me at my home. Really, you know it seemed like this was meant to happen— just meeting each other on the path, then chatting about old times, and how we used to run into each other at baseball games with our kids, etc. Like I said—it felt comfortable, yes, that's it. So I told him he could call me sometime—maybe for lunch or coffee."

"In other words, you fell for it," she said with laughter in her voice. Sarah has an infectious laugh, and suddenly we burst into laughter simultaneously, causing the men at the bar to glance over at us.

"Seriously, though, Sarah, it was the day after Christmas. Sort of a depressing day! That day never passes for me without some sadness invading my thoughts for awhile. You know that's the day Norm died."

"Oh, that's right, so maybe this guy cheered you up a bit?"

"Well, I don't know about that, but yes, I guess it lightened my mood. Like I said—it felt comfortable, a familiar old face!"

"O.K. I got it, it felt good, but tell me, what's he look like? I know he was healthy looking; what else?"

"Honestly, when I saw him coming down the path, even before I recognized him, I thought, this is a good-looking man. And the next moment I realized that I knew him. He's tall, quite attractive—has hair—lots of white hair, and he's lean and clean! It was great—he knew who I was immediately—and after all these years. As I keep saying I liked the attention and the compliments he gave me. Besides that, I had known him almost twenty-five years ago."

"I know, I know," said Sarah, buttering a morsel of French bread, "and I like that—lean and clean—you know, I like a man to be lean, no paunch. So tell me what happened?"

"Well, a few days later he called, and he didn't suggest lunch or dinner, said he just wanted to come and see me."

"And you said, 'Sure, come on over,' didn't you? I know you! So then what happened?"

"Well, he came into my condo and just plopped down on my sofa. It was the darndest thing! Almost immediately he started talking about how much he needed love. I offered him a glass of wine. It was after dinner, and you know I like a little port. But he refused, said he didn't want anything, but then he said to me, 'You go ahead and have what you want, though.' You know, Sarah, very quickly I began to feel stupid."

"Why?" asked Sarah. "Was it something he said, or did? What happened so quickly?"

"Well, I did pour myself a glass of port, and we sat on my sofa chatting for about fifteen minutes. Turns out he really is still married, lives with his wife, but she has bad arthritis. We talked about our kids, and baseball and football. He used to be a football player himself—talked about that, too—but suddenly he took my hand and said, 'Let's go lie on your bed.'"

"No!" said Sarah. "Just like that?"

"Yes, my friend, just like that! I couldn't believe it! D'you realize that's why he wanted to come see me? And do you know, I was tempted—."

"I know, I know; that's what I was thinking." Sarah laughed, looked toward the men at the bar, and whispered, "Go on—go on—so did you go to bed with him?"

With my elbow on the table, my forehead resting on the palm of my hand, I shook with laughter. I looked over at Sarah, facing me in the same position, head bowed and shoulders vibrating. We stopped laughing only to take an occasional breath. Finally I eked out a "No, Sarah, no I didn't."

We came up for air; Sarah wiped her tears away and said, still giggling like a teen-ager, "For a minute, Mary, I thought that's why you called, why you wanted to meet me here at Talbott's. What an anticlimax!"

"Sorry, real sorry, but he's married, and seriously, y'know, in retrospect the whole scene seems pathetic."

"What do you mean, Mary? I guess I kinda know, but go on."

"Well—it sounds like two needy people. Tell me, am I so needy I just fall for anything?"

Sarah waved her hand in the air as she spoke, as though erasing the idea. She has the pretty, fine hand of

a pianist, an artist, which seemed to validate her expertise in these matters. "No, no, it's just that you're kind,
and you like men just like I do. Don't belittle yourself.
But the nerve of that guy!"

"Yes, that's what I thought, but I really felt sorry for
him, apparently starved for love—yet he has a wife."

"So what did you say?" Sarah asked.

"Like I say, mainly I felt stupid, can't even remember
what I said, something about his being married, and—I
don't know—probably even said I'd enjoyed talking with
him, then suggested he go home to his wife. I think he
felt stupid too."

I looked at the menu and asked Sarah, "Have you
decided what you want? I think I'll just have soup."

"That's what I'm having, and some French bread
and this wine is great. Golly, I'm glad you called. This is
such fun—talking about men, I mean."

"I know; isn't it a kick?" I said as the waiter stopped
at our table.

"We just want two soups and French bread," I told
the smiling waiter who seemed to understand that we
weren't too interested in food. He jotted down our order
and moved to the next table. I lifted my wine glass as
though to toast and said, "You know, Sarah, I guess our
hope just springs eternal, and so it goes—on and on—."

That seemed to sum up our confab, but that evening
at home memories surfaced, memories of those years
when I was living alone with our children after their

father died. At first I felt it was just temporary, that this feeling of desolation could not go on very long. There was an incredible vacuum, an emptiness, in my life, in my soul, in my body. And I felt that, in time, my life would include another man. During those early years I wore Norm's ring and talked with him when I went to bed at night. I tried to reassure myself, that "this too will pass."

❦

When I began my job in the school district the change in the course of my life forced a new awareness, that I had only my own inner strength to get through each day. Yet, while accepting the challenge of the job, I continued to believe that somehow my life would get back to normal; deep inside I felt an emptiness that prompted me to believe that this situation was temporary and the void would be filled.

On the first day of my job I was required to attend an orientation meeting in the auditorium of the high school. I sat with new faculty members, next to a handsome young man whose ruddy cheeks and short clipped hair seemed to harmonize with his bursting enthusiasm and eagerness. When he was introduced as a physical education teacher he stood up, smiled, and with humor said a few words about himself. He was at least six feet tall, muscles bulging inside the sleeves of his sportcoat, and I thought he seemed really at ease. But I felt out of place; the smell of the school offices, the hallways, the

classrooms we had toured, and the stuffiness of the auditorium were depressing and tedious. When my name was
called, I hesitated before rising from my seat, so I heard
my name announced again. "Where is our new school
nurse?" the principal asked, and I stood up as in a fog and
said, "Here I am." I heard a little laughter, and as I stood
before everyone the reality came to me; I had a job, and
I would not be going home until the end of the day. Still
there was a part of me that believed things would eventually get back to normal—whatever that was.

Philip, the young physical education teacher who sat
beside me that day of orientation, was the first man since
Norm died who appeared to be genuinely interested in
me and in my family. There was a great difference in our
ages; he was in his twenties, and I was in my late thirties.
Philip had come to work after completing his graduate
work for a teaching credential, and I was beginning a
job, following fifteen years of marriage and five children.

There was a reception for new teachers at a restaurant, Chez Yvonne, on El Camino Real. Again I sat with
Philip and he listened to me talk about my family. He
knew I was concerned about leaving early to watch my
oldest son's football game. Philip assured me that my son
would be all right, that I need not rush home for one
game; there would be others I could attend. But he
watched me fidgeting at the table, checking my watch,
and finally said, "I'll take you out to your car. You need
to do what you want to do, go to that game; you still

have time." There was something about his interest, his understanding, and also his taking me to my car, the physical accompaniment, that gave me a boost. It is one of the little lights in my life that still shines for me, a man who seemed to care and who was helping me.

We became good friends; I did not feel so abandoned. In fact, Philip and I almost had a love affair. Every time we attended a school party at someone's home, he would seek me out, leave the party with me, and we would neck and pet in his car like high school sweethearts. Perhaps if it had been the 1990s I would have succumbed completely, but at that time, my ideals were so well entrenched in my conscience I could not let go. Needless to say, my libido surged and it was difficult to say no to Philip when he would prod me to allow him to visit me in my home. "But I have a houseful of children," I would tell him. Probably his friendship, and his interest in me sexually, bolstered my morale and my sense of wholeness more than any relationship during those first years in the school district.

Human Sexuality was one of the subjects I was responsible for teaching. As the school nurse my charge was to develop curriculum that would inform adolescents about sexuality, yet not stimulate their desire for sexual activity—an almost impossible task. But the assignment did enhance my role as an expert in sexual matters. I believe that the cafeteria conversations, the teasing and insinuations by male teachers would not exist in today's climate because of a possible charge of sexual harassment. Yet I actually enjoyed the flirting that often occurred during the course of my daily duties. Today life has a paradoxical twist: explicit sex is shown in many movies, yet a wayward kiss in the workplace can result in a lawsuit and millions of dollars for the one kissed. In my younger life such films were rare, and flirtation in the workplace was almost routine.

Widows, especially widows with a number of children, are often approached by men with the assumption that their need for sex is great. "After all," I was told many times, and usually by married men, "you have five children, you're accustomed to having sex, and you need me." Perhaps that remark was partly true, but it was love I needed and not just sex. Were men interested only in sex with a woman who had five children?

A friend suggested that I join the adult group for singles at church to brighten up my social life. After I attended several meetings it became clear that only women joined that group. In fact, I quickly dubbed the members of the Single Adult Group as the SAGS, an acronym that seemed appropriate. I recall meeting Theresa, and Charlotte, and Margaret, and all of us sitting on straight chairs in the quiet paneled room. We all watched the open door and then looked away, glancing at each other with amusement, every time we heard high heels clicking down the hallway toward our meeting room. Had we all come there to meet a man? Yes. But we women did become life-long good friends. I have heard that such groups are more successful today if you want to meet men, but I have never returned to find out.

Perhaps a change of career would have provided more opportunities for meeting men, but I discovered early on that it was important to have a job that allowed me the same vacations that my children enjoyed. Once I was almost convinced that I should go to work for an insurance company. The school insurance agent, Les Robb, conferred with me about our school policy and accident claims, and hearing of my own tragic experience regarding insurance coverage, he insisted that I would be an effective salesperson. I had been a victim of a waiting period between my husband's job changes, and was bereft of any life insurance when he died. I knew the value of this protection; life was very difficult not having financial backup when Norm died. Les thought my situation would be a "lead pipe cinch," the sure thing to influence people to buy life insurance. That is one of those roads I did not take. I was tempted because Les said, "You'd have a lot of freedom—your time would be your own, and there are plenty of men in this business—you'd enjoy it." But when he said it would take time to cultivate a clientele and make enough money to live on, I realized I must stay on course; my contract with the school district assured me of a paycheck every month.

Probably the most serious love affair that enriched my life those days and left me with memories that will forever warm my heart and soul was with Coleman, a school superintendent, when I was almost fifty years old. But again the responsibility of so many children, along with other factors, helped diminish the possibility of an enduring relationship. I had known Coleman from years before when my husband and I lived in Stanford Village, the housing facility for married students. We became reacquainted when I met him at a school meeting. Gradually he developed the habit of stopping by my health office to have his blood pressure checked, and to share with me his anxiety and misery during the terminal illness of his wife. He was a thoughtful friend, generous in his praise of my work. "I believe you're too good for this job," he said. "You have talents and ability that should provide you with much more reward both financially and professionally." He made me feel good.

After Coleman's wife died he became not only my best friend but also my lover. One summer I planned a trip to Vermont to visit my sister while my children were at camp. During that time Coleman planned to attend a conference in New York City; he suggested that I fly to New York to spend a few days with him. It was my first opportunity for such freedom, and my mother hastened to cheer me on, eager for me to have a romance, and possibly another husband. She sent me a nightgown, post haste, a short chiffon, electric blue, lacy gown, super sexy, unlike any I had ever worn. Its label was *Vanity Fair.* (I must confess it has been in a bureau drawer ever since, because it was a time to remember. How I laughed at myself recently, when I found it tucked away, and realized that I had never discarded it.)

I have in my mind images of that rendezvous: Coleman and I at Radio City Music Hall, holding hands, watching the dancers and listening to the music. But most memorable is the feeling of belonging, of being with a man who loved me; for the first time in years I felt the warmth of being one of the many couples in the audience. So often I had been alone or with other women in a theater or music hall, and had felt out of sync. On the screen of my mind's video I not only see and hear the dancers and the music, but I feel an indescribable sense of completeness, a kind of bliss. I have not experienced that feeling since then.

After the New York rendezvous Coleman wrote me letters whenever he left town on business or to visit relatives. They were letters of reflection and deep feeling, like poetry which one memorizes. And he wrote letters to me, without leaving town, from his home, only blocks away. He had been slow to recover from a depression when his wife died but gradually his vigor and interest in life was revived. At times he mentioned his upbringing in a Mormon household, and one time he indicated that he felt a different kind of freedom with me.

One afternoon toward the end of the school year, Coleman seemed out of character when he opened his highest kitchen cupboard and brought out a bottle of

J and B Scotch. It was half full. I knew he and his wife had been teetotalers, and I had never had an alcoholic drink with Coleman, not even in New York.

"Coleman, I didn't know you had liquor in your house," I said. "Oh, yes," he said, "there's nothing the matter with this. I like to have a drink once in awhile." He took out a couple of glasses, and asked if I wanted soda or water with it. Abruptly the mood in our surroundings had changed, and I said, "I'll have plain water, but only a whisper of Scotch; in fact, I like it only to flavor the water." He laughed, and fixed my light drink before making a hefty Scotch and water for himself. We went into his living room where he put on a record. "It's an old song," he said. It was something about "Mary in the morning," a song I had never heard. I felt as though I were taking part in something that was not real. "This's a side of you I've never seen before," I said, watching him swirl the ice around in his drink, "and I thought you didn't drink alcohol, Coleman. I thought your religion didn't approve." He smiled sheepishly, rather impishly, like a boy getting away with something that was forbidden.

"You know, sometimes I just like to get out of the saddle," he said. He sat on the sofa, holding his glass with both hands, elbows on his knees, and studied me as I sat in a chair across from him.

"You don't miss a thing, do you? You're always thinking," he said, like he was scolding me. But in the next moment he said, "You know what I'd really like to do? I'd like to sack all of this, the school job, this house, the whole bit, and just get in my racer with you and take off!"

"I know," I said, and for an evanescent moment I shared his fantasy, but it floated away as quickly as it had surfaced. I stayed on course, came to my senses, and said to Coleman, in the "take charge" voice I often used to talk to my children, "But that isn't what you're going to do, at least not today or tomorrow." I removed his glass from his hand. He let go willingly, and followed me into the kitchen and watched while I poured the drinks down the drain. "Scotch isn't a good idea right now," I said.

"That's so true," Coleman said, a silly smile on his face. "Like I said, you're always thinking."

Somehow I had been caught up in an illusion, almost separated from reality, when he poured the Scotch into glasses. But when I saw the reckless abandon in Coleman's eyes I came down to earth; it was as though he was mesmerized by the ice swirling in the amber fluid. Thank heavens, I had caught myself. Those few minutes of histrionics were a revelation for me; I perceived his fragility, his struggle with internal forces.

Feeling my own two feet on the ground, I reminded him, "You have an important meeting this evening, and I need to get home and make dinner for my family—that's how things really are, Coleman." I took my car

keys out of my purse and opened the front door.
Together we walked to my car, and he said, "Thanks for
bringing over the boxes. You're such a big help." (That
had been my reason for being there in the first place;
Coleman had told me at the beginning of the week that
he needed boxes in order to start packing for his move
to Utah when school was out. I still had Bekin boxes in
my garage from several years ago when our family
moved from Palos Verdes, so I had offered to drop them
off at his house.) He did not embrace me or kiss me as I
prepared to get in my car; as always he was afraid the
neighbors might be watching.

I stopped at the Lucky Store on my way home to
pick up hot dogs and chili, and salad stuff, amazed at the
power implicit in one's pursuit of essential tasks; it not
only nurtured and maintained my family but also kept
me on course.

A few weeks after the Scotch incident, Coleman
asked me to stop by his house for lunch. "Finally I think
I'm over the hump," he said. "I had a good board meeting last night." We ate deli sandwiches and drank Cokes
at his kitchen table; he was in good spirits. But when I
was leaving he brought out two bottles from his medicine cabinet and held them up so I could read the labels,
Valium and Seconal. They were large bottles, like a

supply of 100s. "These are what keep me going," he said, "the white ones to calm me during the day, and the red ones to help me sleep at night."

"Good Lord, Coleman," I said, "where'd you get so many pills?"

"Don't be alarmed," he said. "It's all right. I get them from my doctor friend across the street." He opened the Valium bottle, shook out two or three pills, and tossed them into his mouth.

"You don't take them like that, Coleman," I said. "You're eating them as though they were peanuts!"

"Don't worry, dear, don't worry; the doctor says they won't cause any harm," he said as he replaced the bottles in his medicine cabinet.

Not only had Coleman had a lack of confidence and decisiveness concerning his job lately, but also his letters to me were laden with questions about his ability to carry on, and misgivings about himself. After seeing his supply of pills, and the nonchalance associated with his use of drugs, I called his doctor friend and neighbor to make certain his medication was well supervised. "You need not worry," the doctor said. "I'm right across the street, and he's doing fine."

Coleman's letters to me revealed a premonition that I would not be interested in a long-term relationship with him. And it was true that my own busy life made it impossible for me to spend the time with Coleman that was necessary to nurture such a commitment. I had a pervasive sense of being in limbo; I wanted to be with Coleman yet I questioned my willingness to embark on a voyage in an entirely different direction. I felt tossed about in a pool of uncertainty. In a letter to me, during a time in which one of my sons had been seriously injured in a motorcycle accident, he wrote: "Please tell your sons I enjoyed dinner with them and you *very* much and I hope Norm is much better and able to walk without any difficulty. My visits to your place and with you are without question the best and most worthwhile of *any* experiences. I will always look at them with immense gratitude, remembering the order and love in your house among you all, the great lightning storms on the beach, and, of course, your gracious company."

Another time he wrote, "I truly hope our friendship, begun many years ago, will continue, even though—and Mary, I'm probably dead wrong—I thought our conversation last night was definitely lacking the intangible requirement which relationships of a special kind must *have* to survive." His last letter to me seemed to foretell my future: "Your constancy and caring during this long year of my recovery will always be a most precious memory, Mary. You have understood where others have not—you have traveled the same road and you certainly have won over imposing odds. And you will continue to preside over a family of four sons and a daughter called

Mary in a satisfying and rewarding way. This, as I see it (and to use a Mormon expression), is to be your greatest 'calling,' and your first and primary love."

At the end of the next school year, our relationship ended. I had just come home from school and was busy in the kitchen preparing supper for my children when a car drove into my driveway. Through the kitchen window I recognized Coleman's son, Grant, a tall blond young man. His navy blue sport coat hung from his broad shoulders with a casual elegance, and I watched him straighten his tie and pat it in place over his white shirt as he stepped over the bicycles lying on the concrete walkway by my kitchen door. Coleman had described Grant, the middle child of three sons, as "a young Turk—he knows how to make money—not even thirty years old and he's made his first million." The tone of his voice had suggested a mixture of a father's pride, almost arrogance, and a dash of disdain.

I had known Grant when our children were young and he baby-sat for my oldest son. Now he lived in another state but had come to town apparently to help his father arrange his personal matters regarding retirement and his future life. Grant clapped his hands, held them together, and looking as though he was initiating a business deal, he said, "Mrs. Shaw, my brothers and I think my father should get married, and he tells us that you are Number One on the Hit Parade." As he spoke, two of my sons arrived from school and came into the kitchen with their friends looking for food. Mary with her best friend, Monica, walked up the driveway. Suddenly my house was overflowing with children.

"And where is he?" I asked, bewildered and surprised by Grant's sudden announcement. My hands were busy, molding a meatloaf into shape, "Why is Coleman not here talking about this?"

Grant laughed, shrugged his shoulders, and said, "Well, I can see you really have your hands full. Did I come at the wrong time?"

"Oh, no," I said, "this's fine, Grant; I've just got to get dinner started. But something's missing in this conversation. Is this a proposal? I need to talk to Coleman." I stopped to think for a minute. "No," I said, "I mean—he needs to talk to me."

I put several potatoes, one by one, around the meatloaf and slid the pan into the oven. Grant watched me, and after I washed my hands and dried them on a towel, I turned to him and said, "Grant, what's this about anyway? Are you taking care of your father? Making his decisions?" Grant was suddenly uncomfortable. "Oh, no, it isn't that. It's just that he thinks so much of you, and my brothers thought I should come and see you."

Mary and Monica had bypassed the kitchen to go back to her room; we could hear their laughter echoing in the hallway.

"You know, Grant," I said, "I have five children and Coleman has been here many times for dinner. He knows it isn't that simple. I have great responsibilities."

"Oh, I know, I know," Grant said, as if he understood, and perhaps had made a mistake or asked the wrong question. "Well, I'd better go, this's a busy place."

He looked around my kitchen, turned to me, and at the same time reached for the knob of the kitchen door. "Well, I can see it's true; you really have your hands full, and I do have to go." As he opened the door and walked outside he said, "You certainly have a nice family, Mrs. Shaw."

I watched him walk down my driveway, hop into his Mercedes, and click the door closed. He waved as he drove away. Yes, I thought, Coleman was right. His son Grant is a businessman; he came to research the market, sensed it was a poor venture, and that was that.

Coleman never called me. A few weeks later I read in the local newspaper the announcement of his engagement to his long-time secretary. (She must have been Number Two on the Hit Parade.) I wondered if Grant had informed his father that I was not interested in marriage, that "her hands are full of her family."

But near tragedy struck the following week. I read in the local newspaper that Coleman had been admitted to the hospital with an overdose of drugs, an apparent suicide. When I went to the hospital to see him, his sons informed me that he could not have visitors. Later in the week I received a call from Grant and was able to visit

Coleman to say hello and wish him well, with his future wife at his side. He appeared helpless, sadness emanating from the depths of his pale blue eyes. He reached for my hand, held it briefly, and nodded when I wished him a speedy recovery. "Take care of yourself," he said, lifting his hand in a small wave. And it was my turn to nod and wave goodbye.

Again the newspaper kept me informed; I read the account of Coleman's wedding and his move to Utah. The last time I heard from him was a phone call from San Francisco when he changed planes en route to Japan. I picked up the phone in my health office and heard his slurred words. "Just wanted to say hello, and ask how you're doing," he said. I could not answer, and then he continued, coughing and clearing his voice. I recognized a familiar tone in his voice, puffed up with the vigor and spirit I liked about him when he let go of his image and could be himself. "This's not the way it should be," he almost shouted. "I hate this damned retirement, these stupid tours. You and I should be driving around in my racer! How the hell did this happen?"

I said, "I don't know, Coleman, but that's the way it is." I told him I hoped he had a good trip and wished him well. I hung up the phone and thought about the many years he had acted the part expected of him. Probably I was one of the few who really knew him, his true self, those times he discarded his image and became real. I recalled the time he reached for the violin of his youth and played with abandonment. "I used to play this when I was a boy," he said to me as he returned it to its case. He had had it restrung at a local music shop so he could play for me. We shared moments of pure joy. Forever I will cherish the memories. But it was clear to me that my river of life had its own course, and I knew I must stay with it. Grant and his brothers had apparently responded to their "calling"; they looked after their father.

❧

As years went by I often felt as though my own life was on hold; I was continuously marking time, anticipating less family responsibility. I thought that eventually I would be able to pursue activities that would broaden my horizon and perhaps include some interesting men. We lived in a family-oriented neighborhood with working fathers, often commuting to San Francisco, mothers at home, PTA, block parties, and an abundance of children.

I was the only single parent amidst many couples, except for Joe, a widower, who lived two streets away. We would see each other at neighborhood gatherings, and periodically he would suggest that we get together sometime. His children were in college and he was alone. Joe told me that he had "these cyclical urges" and that perhaps we could make some arrangement for me to go over to his house on those occasions to make love. I thought he was kidding and made light of his remark. "Never heard of such a condition," I told him, "but I do like to play dominoes." He continued to pay attention to me at parties, and I decided that I would like to get to know him better. Joe came by my house one evening while I was in my garage doing the laundry.

"How about it?" he said. "How about coming over for a drink?"

"I really haven't time; I need to finish all this laundry," I said.

"Big deal," he said. "After all, you do have a washer and dryer! Doesn't that do all the work?"

In spite of his thoughtless comment I decided to accept his invitation. I turned on the dryer with the last load of wash, closed my garage, and walked over to his house with him. Nothing ventured, nothing gained; you need to have some fun, I told myself. He mixed me a Scotch so strong I couldn't drink it and encouraged me to sit close to him on his family room sofa. It occurred to me that he might be serious about his "cyclical urge."

So I asked him if that was what this social encounter was all about. "Is that why I'm here?" I asked. "I didn't know you were serious when you mentioned your physical time clock, Joe."

"Of course I was; don't tell me you want to go back to your garage and finish your laundry," he said, laughing as he tried to slide his hand under my sweater.

"Yes, Joe," I said, "that's what I want to do. I want to go home and finish my laundry." I walked home, amazingly calm, knowing that I need spend no more time thinking about Joe. I opened my garage door. The dryer had completed *its* cycle, and I carried my clean laundry into the kitchen to fold. Truly there *is* solace in mundane tasks; losing one's self to find one's self. Finding one's self and getting the clean laundry folded and put away at the same time is a grand coup play.

❦

My children came of age in the sixties and early seventies, while I continued to work in a high school district. As they became involved in their own pursuits and relationships, I began to have more freedom to reach beyond work and family. At first I mixed business with pleasure, traveling to Paris where I attended the International Conference of Health Education, and even danced in the ballroom at Versailles. This led to an invitation to the meeting in London in 1979 where I delivered a paper on high school health education curriculum at Royal Festival Hall.

There was a new lightness in my life and I joined a doubles group in tennis at the Foothills Tennis Club where my children had learned the sport. I became a serious golfer, along with a friend, Dina Bolla, who was the owner of a travel agency. She invited me to her condo in Kauai where we played the best golf of our lives at Princeville, and found incredible refreshment in the rain forest. We also golfed on the finest courses in

California, and in places like Cancun, Mexico, until Dina married and later moved to Switzerland, her homeland.

A few years ago I visited Dina in Locarno. We climbed high into the Alps where a magnificent mountain stood alone—yet one of many—snow-capped. I watched water gushing forth from a myriad of jets into one great stream down the mountainside, and felt the might of the moving water.

Throughout my life I have found solace in aloneness, which I believe strengthens relationships; to be at peace with one's self makes it possible to be at peace with others. And I shall continue to "celebrate the possible," while I value and cherish my independence. I had a dear friend, a neighbor across the street, who called me one day, years ago, to tell me that he had read about a good vintage year for a particular Louis M. Martini wine. "Let's buy a case and split it," Sam said, "put it away for several years and we'll have a fine old wine." It sounded like a good idea; we drove to the liquor store, bought the case of 1970 Louis Martini Cabernet Sauvignon, and I stored my six bottles. I laid them in the bottom of a closet, the coolest place in my house. I decided to keep this special wine until I got married again. Then I forgot about it. That wine is now twenty-six years old. Finally I realize that being alone may not be temporary. Perhaps the reward is simply a glass of fine vintage wine.